CONSIDER
THE LILIES

CONSIDER THE LILIES

A PLEA FOR CREATIONAL THEOLOGY

T. M. MOORE

PUBLISHING
P.O. BOX 817 • PHILLIPSBURG • NEW JERSEY 08865-0817

All quotations by Gerard Manley Hopkins are from W. H. Gardner, ed., *Poems and Prose of Gerard Manley Hopkins* (London: Penguin Books, 1985).

All quotations by William Cowper are from James Robert Boyd, ed., *The Task, Table Talk, and Other Poems of William Cowper* (New York: A. S. Barnes & Co., 1857).

The poem "Logos" was first published in *Theology Today*, January 2003. Used by permission.

All Scripture quotations are from the King James Version, unless otherwise indicated.

Page design and typesetting by Lakeside Design Plus

Printed in the United States of America

Library of Congress Cataloging-in-Publication Data
Moore, T. M. (Terry Michael), 1949–
    Consider the lilies : a plea for creational theology / T.M. Moore.
        p.   cm.
    Includes bibliographical references and indexes.
    ISBN-13: 978-0-87552-716-1 (paper)
    ISBN-10: 0-87552-716-7 (paper)
        1. Revelation. 2. God. 3. Theology, Doctrinal. 4. Edwards, Jonathan, 1703–1758.
    I. Title.

BT127.3.M66 2005
231.7—dc22
                                                                    2005042989

CONTENTS

INTRODUCTION

God's Grandeur

The world is charged with the grandeur of God.
　　It will flame out, like shining from shook foil;
　　It gathers to a greatness, like the ooze of oil
Crushed. Why do men then now not reck his rod?
Generations have trod, have trod, have trod;
　　And all is seared with trade; bleared, smeared with toil;
　　And wears man's smudge and shares man's smell: the soil
Is bare now, nor can foot feel, being shod.

And for all this, nature is never spent;
　　There lives the dearest freshness deep down things;
And though the last lights off the black West went
　　Oh, morning, at the brown brink eastward, springs—
Because the Holy Ghost over the bent
　　World broods with warm breast and with ah! bright wings.

　　　　　　　　　　　　　　　—Gerard Manley Hopkins

A Glory Ignored but Persistent

With remarkable insight and economy of words, nineteenth-century British poet Gerard Manley Hopkins declared in this unforgettable sonnet truths that every generation of believers in the God of

7

the Bible has acknowledged: In the works of His hands God is revealing His glory and grandeur. Sometimes it surprises us, flaming out for an instant only to recede again into what we normally regard as the commonplace. At other times it seems to ooze around us, gathering strength and power, rich and fragrant, filling the place we occupy with an unmistakable sense of the divine presence. So powerful, so undeniable can be the sense of God's self-disclosure that it is remarkable that most people seem to take so little notice of these evidences of divine glory and grandeur. Occupied with the affairs of this world, they trudge through their daily routines of trade and toil, unmindful of the glory shimmering and beckoning around them. They take the creation for granted, or even abuse it. Having shod their feet with the comforts of material existence, they surfeit themselves with an abundance of things, preferring these for their own sake alone, rather than for any firsthand experience of God revealing Himself in what He has made.

Undeterred, "nature"—a term whose validity we will at length consider—continues to pour forth glory and grandeur, deep, dear, fresh and new each day, in a recurring display that is as persistent and utterly regular as day following night. This exhibition of the divine presence is the work of the Holy Spirit, who broods over the creation, warming and renewing it day by day, nurturing and sustaining it so that it manifests the grandeur of God and shows forth His glory in ways that provoke us to wonder, reverence, and delight.

A Glory to Be Perceived and Experienced?

Hopkins's poem raises some important questions: If God is, indeed, revealing Himself in the things of creation, as even the Scriptures attest (e.g., Ps. 19:1–6), what kinds of expression does that grandeur take? May we perceive and experience it? If so, where, and how will we recognize it when we do? In what forms should we expect to encounter it? By what means? And what can it tell us about God or His plans, purposes, truth, or ways? Why do so many people, including those who claim to know God, seem unable to see God's grandeur in the things He has made? How can we remain so curiously indifferent to it? How is it that the searing, smearing, blearing life of toil and things continues to divert the gaze and enthrall the affections and energies of so many people? Why can Hopkins see the grandeur of God, experience His presence, and report it so eloquently and convincingly? How does he know this to be a work of the Spirit of God? Is it possible for ordinary folk such as we are to see God's grandeur as well, and if so, what difference might it make? How should we respond to such revelation?

A Capacious Reservoir of Means

Hopkins does not answer these questions for us. It is not the vocation of poets to explain; rather, their calling is to provoke awareness, engage our minds, and stimulate our affections, and this they have faithfully done throughout the centuries. Nearly a hundred years before Hopkins, English poet William Cowper made observations similar to his. Cowper saw the creation as a "capacious reservoir of means" that God has prepared to aid us in furthering His will. The poet called his readers to discipline their seeing and to seek understanding of Him in creation. But Cowper also advised us to seek out counselors to help discern the ways of God in the things He has made:

> What is his creation less
> Than a capacious reservoir of means
> Form'd for his use, and ready at his will?
> Go, dress thine eyes with eye-salve; ask of him,
> Or ask of whomsoever he has taught;
> And learn, though late, the genuine cause of all.
>
> —*The Task*, 2.203–5

Like Hopkins, Cowper encourages us to think that we might actually be able to discern the hand of God in the things He has made, and to discover through the means of creation something more of His being, purposes, truth, and ways. But in order to do so, we must "dress [our] eyes with eye-salve." We must learn to look, study to see clearly, and take the time to investigate this "capacious reservoir." We may appeal to God Himself, as well as to those He has shown how to discern His glory in the creation around, so that, leaning on His instruction and following their example and guidance, we also might learn, though late in life, to observe God's grandeur and celebrate His presence and the work of His Spirit in all He has made and sustains.

It is reasonable to expect that if we could discern the self-disclosure of God in the things He has made, and if we would take the time to do so with greater regularity, we also might experience more of the sense of wonder, reverence, and delight that infuses the last line of Hopkins's poem. If we could learn to see in all things Him who is the "genuine cause" of all, and learn to know Him better, we might be more given to praise, thanksgiving, confidence, joy, and hope throughout all our days.

Toward a Richer, Fuller Experience of God

In our day, as so often in the past, learned counselors are offering helpful instruction concerning what we might expect to see of God's grandeur in the things He has made—the creation all around us, the elements of culture, and the actions of conscience expressed in the ways of people with one another. From their work we can be encouraged to believe that we, too, can penetrate to the revelation of God in creation, culture, and the conscience with eyes to see what God might be showing us there. With them we can discover a deeper, richer, more wonder-filled and continuous relationship with God. We can train our eyes to see, our ears to hear, our minds to discern, and our hearts to delight in the flamings and oozings of that capacious reservoir of glory and grandeur. And we can find our reading and study of Scripture, the touchstone of all divine revelation, come to greater brilliance and intensity as our experience of God in creation reinforces His revelation of Himself in His Word.

10

The Plan of This Book

The purpose of this little volume is to reexamine the biblical doctrine of general revelation from the perspective of what I refer to as *creational theology*. The specific meaning of this term, and the reasons for employing it, will be made clear at length. While this is a book on theology, it is not intended primarily for theologians. Rather, I hope to encourage church leaders and members with some introductory instruction in how they might improve their relationship with God by learning to *do* theology as part of their everyday lives.

The course of our study will unfold as follows: In part 1, which consists of one chapter, we will explore the meaning of *theology* as something other than an academic discipline, or the literary products of such a discipline. Theology, we will see, is not merely something we read or study; it is something we *do* for the purpose of growing in the knowledge of and love for God. As something we do, theology presents six windows through which we may observe God's self-revelation as we master the skills and disciplines of looking upon the glory of God. One of those windows, the focus of our study, is creational theology.

Next, in part 2, we will explore the doctrine of general revelation, especially as this doctrine has been championed by representatives of the Reformed theological community. We will try to understand the essential teachings of the Reformed doctrine of general revelation, together with ways in which those teachings have been *mis*used over the years, and some explanation as to why they stand in such *dis*use among believers today. Our objective will be to reinforce the biblical teaching concerning general revelation, and to encourage the hope that we today might be able to explore this "capacious reservoir" of divine means to enhance our relationship with God.

Yet in order to realize that end, we will need grounding in the biblical teaching on the subject of general revelation. We will turn to this in chapter 3, where we will investigate in somewhat more detail the teaching of Scripture concerning general revelation, in order to gain a sense of how God in His Word guides us to consider, understand, and use His revelation of Himself in His world.

From there we will turn to a consideration of creational theology as a particular approach to making valid use of the doctrine of general revelation (chapter 4). It is my conviction, following that of Reformed theologians from the past, that general revelation is true and reliable revelation. Yet if we are to avoid the misuses and mistakes of the past (and present) with respect to this revelation, we must follow the guidelines that Scripture itself prescribes. In so doing, we enter into the practice of creational theology as a vital tool of theological improvement and spiritual growth.

In part 3 we will examine what we have discussed about the subject of creational theology in the light of the teaching and practice of one of the greatest creational theologians of all time, the New England Puritan Jonathan Edwards (chapters 5 and 6). We will investigate Edwards's extensive use of the doctrine of general revelation, and recommend his example as a guide for thinking further about how to practice creational theology in our day.

In the last section, part 4 (chapters 7–9), we will consider how to develop the skills and disciplines that will enable us to look out the window of creational theology and perceive and experience the glory of God. Following Edwards, I will offer some suggestions for beginning to make better use of the revelation of God in creation, culture, and conscience for the acknowledgment and advancement of His glory. Throughout I will provide questions for additional study or discussion, as well as activities to engage in so as to begin learning the skills of creational theology for the purposes of spiritual growth. An annotated bibliography at the end of the book provides resources for further study of this exciting subject.

We will also have additional recourse to the poems of Gerard Manley Hopkins and to William Cowper's *The Task*. These two Christian poets, from two different traditions, can provoke us to greater curiosity, encourage us with their insights, and urge us on in our quest to make better use of the revelation of God in the things He has made. Along the way, we will also draw on the comments and observations of others to encourage us in the value and practice of this vital theological discipline. As I will argue in chapter 1, theological studies often result in theological *products*—books, courses, and so forth. The same is true of the study of general revelation, which is once again receiving attention from theologians and others, many of whose works I will draw from in the pages that follow. One of the glories of creational theology is that it encourages different kinds of theological products— musical compositions, paintings, stories and novels, rich conversation, and poetry. While these can be somewhat more challenging to create and interpret than theological narratives in the form of books, papers, courses, and seminars, they can be equally valid, and even more useful in certain ways, in fostering knowledge of and love for God. In my own practice of creational theology, poetry has proved a useful means of recording my perceptions and capturing my experiences of God's self-disclosure in creation, and of making permanent the impressions and significance of those experiences. Therefore, with the reader's indulgence, I will include along the way examples of my own meditations on the glory and grandeur of God as I have experienced His flaming and oozing around me from time to time.

Acknowledgments and Purpose

I would like to thank Allan Fisher, Thom Notaro, and the staff at P&R Publishing for their encouragement in this project and their boldness in being willing to bring it to print. I further wish to thank the board and staff of the Jonathan Edwards Institute, and especially Pedro Govantes, the Institute's director, for the opportunity of presenting a portion of this book in the form of lectures at the Institute's 2002 annual conference. In recent years, this little platoon of visionaries has done much to advance the purposes that this volume promotes. And I want to thank my wife, Susie, for putting up with, encouraging, and even joining in certain of my many sorties into the field of creational theology over the years, and helping me to sort out my thinking on this subject. In addition, her editorial assistance has been invaluable in the completion of this project. It is to her, with deepest gratitude and love, that this present volume is dedicated.

13

My purpose is to help readers, especially those in the Reformed tradition, to become aware of what for most contemporary Christians is a significant lacuna in their theological studies and spiritual lives. I want to challenge you to take seriously the revelation of God in creation, and to begin to enter more fully and more consistently into the discovery and celebration of God's glory that is being manifested there. As Cowper reminds us, a vast neglected realm of revelation awaits us, which only a few consider:

> Nature, enchanting Nature, in whose form
> And lineaments divine I trace a hand
> That errs not, and find raptures still renew'd,
> Is free to all men—universal prize.
> Strange that so fair a creature should yet want
> Admirers, and be destined to divide
> With meaner objects e'en the few she finds!
>
> —*The Task*, 3.721–27

It is that "fair creature," that "universal prize" that we want to learn how to admire and enjoy by taking up the happy task of creational theology, and beginning to "trace a hand / that errs not, and find raptures still renew'd."

PART 1

THROUGH WINDOWS
OF GLORY

Ambassadors of Glory
Psalm 19:1–6

They're speaking to us. All created things
ambassadors of glory are to ears
indifferent to their glad reports. The spears
and arrows which commercial culture slings
against us deafen us. Their welcome stings
and stabs distort our hearing. Business sears
our eager eardrums; entertainment blears
audition with the piper's tunes it sings.
The echo of banality so rings
within us hardly anybody hears
creation's message. Whether joy or tears,
we take scant notice of the word it brings.
  Throw up a shield around my ears, O Lord,
  and let me hear creation's glorious word!

1

THE INESCAPABLE, INEVITABLE TASK

For now we see through a glass, darkly; but then face to face: now I know in part; but then shall I know even as also I am known.
—1 Corinthians 13:12

Authentic Christian faith always inclines one toward understanding the God who has claimed our lives.
—Stanley J. Grenz and Roger E. Olson[1]

Doing, Not Just Reading

"So, tell me: Who are some of your favorite theologians?"

I should have anticipated this question, but it settled on me like a cold chill. This was my first interview for my first calling in ministry as a fresh seminary graduate. I was seeking a position in Christian education at a well-known church, and this interview with the pastor was part of the application process. It had been going swimmingly, I thought, as he and I chatted about my views on Christian education, evangelism, the spiritual life, and so forth. Then this question came out of nowhere.

I wanted to say to him, "Actually, I don't like reading theology very much. It strikes me as so dry and abstract, so locked into definitions, syllogisms, deductions, and conclusions. So detached from life. In fact, I find it rather boring; so I don't read that much theology." Which would have been true. But I had read *some* theology, and what I had read was, I knew, important, even if I had not found it terribly interesting. So I put forth a few names of some theologians with whose works I was at least somewhat familiar—Augustine, Luther, Calvin, Kuyper, Thielicke, and one or two others. The pastor seemed pleased. And I was greatly relieved that he did not ask me to elaborate on precisely what it was about each of these theologians that I appreciated.

That was over twenty-five years ago, and my view of reading theology has not changed much since then. Oh, I have read a great deal more theology over the years, and, I hope, with greater appreciation. But I still find it tedious and tiring. Maybe theology is an acquired taste. If so, how much of it does one have to sample before beginning to delight in it? Or perhaps the ability to grasp subtle theological arguments and draw them out in concise conclusions and subtle implications is genetic. Regardless, either I haven't acquired the taste or I don't have the gene. Reading theology continues to be one of my least favorite, least rewarding, and most demanding activities. I read theology, to be sure, but not with the relish—or confidence—I might like.

At the same time, doing theology—as opposed to reading it—has come to be the most exciting, most intellectually stimulating, and most spiritually uplifting activity I know. That is, over the years I have come to see that growing in knowledge of, love for, and communion with God through all the means by which He is revealing Himself is the most wonderful privilege and exciting adventure in which anyone could be involved. Doing theology is a most satisfying and rewarding enterprise, a happy task indeed. And doing theology—including doing creational theology—is the high privilege, inescapable duty, and inevitable calling of everyone who names the name of Jesus Christ.

18

But if we are to appreciate the value and enter into the joy and excitement of doing theology, we need to make sure we understand just what this discipline entails, and what opportunities for doing theology are available to us. In particular, before we take up the happy task of doing creational theology, we must first make sure that we understand the nature of the theological task itself, and be persuaded of its relevance for our lives.

Doing Theology unto the Knowledge of God

How is it simultaneously possible for one to find *reading* theology so tedious and difficult and *doing* theology the most exciting thing in his life?

A Traditional Understanding: Theology as Account

For me, it's a matter of understanding the nature and purpose of theology, and of learning to employ all the disciplines of theological studies according to their proper place and for their proper ends. As traditionally understood, *theology* is defined as the setting forth of a systematic understanding of the biblical teaching about God. As Gerhard Ebeling puts it, "The common presupposition is that theology involves a reflected account of the Christian faith."[2] This is not a very involved or detailed definition of theology, but it provides a good place to start. In this view, theology is an account, a reflection—in writing or teaching—of one's experience of or conclusions about God and what it means to believe in Him. The important point is that *theology* as understood here is an account, that is, something written or spoken, that reflects the theological views of a particular individual. This is a valid definition, as far as it goes, and will be true at least in part for our work in creational theology as well.

The Traditional View Improved

Herman Hoeksema offers a more traditional and more specific definition of theology or, to use his term, *dogmatics*:

> Dogmatics is that theological discipline in which the dogmatician, in organic connection with the church in the past as well as in the present, purposes to elicit from the Scriptures the true knowledge of God, to set forth the same in systematic form, and, after comparison of the existing dogmas with Scripture, to bring the knowledge of God to a higher state of development.[3]

Note that Hoeksema, like Ebeling, sees the finished work of theology as some kind of verbal product, something that is "set forth," presumably in writing or speaking and in a systematic (or logical) form, such as a book or lecture. But Hoeksema's definition offers three improvements over Ebeling's.

1. He grounds theology in the Scriptures. Theology's primary source and principal substance is not the perceptions or experiences of the theologian—the "reflection" of one who labors in theological studies—but the revelation of God in His Word. This is an important principle that we will need to keep in mind and practice carefully as we take up the work of creational theology. While all theology will necessarily reflect the biases, experiences, and inclinations of individual theologians, any theological work can be only partial and incomplete, and runs the risk of being downright wrong, apart from grounding in the Word of God. All our theological views, opinions, and conclusions must, as Hoeksema observes, be compared with the Scriptures in order to determine the degree of their truthfulness (2 Tim. 3:15–17; Acts 17:11). Scripture is both the starting point and touchstone of all proper theological activity, of all we do in seeking to bring our knowledge of God "to a higher state of development," including the work of creational theology.

2. Hoeksema acknowledges that theology is a communal activity. We should not undertake the work of theology in isolation from the rest of the Christian community, past and present, far and wide. Our theologizing, in other words, must be carried out in a dialogue with others of our contemporaries who are doing the work of theology, as well as with those in the past who have worked in this area—and that across a very broad spectrum of those who, wrestling with the teaching of God's Word, have devoted themselves to increasing the

20

knowledge of God among His people. As we will see, this is true as well for our work in creational theology. Theology is not a matter of merely private interpretation or opinion. Theology will be most useful for achieving its overarching purpose to the degree that it is both grounded in Scripture and carried out in dialogue with the entire Christian community.

3. Hoeksema improves on Ebeling's definition by pointing to the proper end of theology, namely, the knowledge of God. Theology is not an end in itself. The *study* of theology is not an end in itself. Theology, the reading and study of theology, and every other way that we might *do* theology are for the purpose of knowing God better. We will have more to say concerning this in due course, so let me just leave it at this for now, noting again that the knowledge of God is or ought to be the proper end of theology, as Hoeksema observes in his definition of dogmatics.

Theology and the Knowledge of Humankind

But as Calvin reminds us in the opening words of the *Institutes*, knowing God—which is the proper object of theological studies— necessarily involves us in seeking a more intimate knowledge of ourselves. John Frame, echoing Calvin, writes:

> In knowing God, we come to know His relations to the world and to many things in the world, especially to ourselves. We cannot know God without understanding some of those relations: the biblical God is the God of the covenant, the Creator and sustainer of the world, the Redeemer and judge of men. So we cannot know God without knowing other things at the same time.[4]

German theologian Helmut Thielicke would seem to agree with Frame, at least insofar as theology touches on the knowledge of humankind as well: "Since God discloses himself to man and seeks to be his God, any statement about God is also a statement about his relation to man. To that degree man is there in every theological utterance and thus gives it an anthropological reference."[5]

21

Thus, in order to truly know God—the proper end of theology—we must also know something about ourselves, about how God relates to us and how we know Him, what makes us unique, how we express or represent ourselves, what our peculiarities as creatures are, what we can discover about our deepest longings and aspirations, how we understand and relate to the creation around us, and what all this tells us about the knowledge of God. The knowledge of God requires, and is brought to a higher level of development by, deeper and more personal knowledge of people as they carry out their lives in the creation God has made.

Theology and the Knowledge of the World

But Frame also mentioned that knowing God involves knowing something about His relations to the world as its Creator and Sustainer. Thus, the task of theology further requires that we pay attention to "many things in the world" and what they might be saying to us about the one who made and sustains them. The disciplines of creational theology can be of great help here, as we will see.

Alexander Schmemann makes a helpful connection between the knowledge of people and the knowledge of the creation as these serve the purposes of theology when he describes man as a priest, whose primary calling, in interaction with the world, is to offer thanksgiving to God:

> The first, the basic definition of man is that he is *the priest*. He stands at the center of the world and unifies it in his act of blessing it to God—and by filling the world with this eucharist, he transforms his life, the one that he receives from the world, unto life in God, into communion with Him.[6]

Note the verbs here: Man *stands* at the center of the world—he is an active observer and participant in the midst of created reality of all kinds. He *unifies* the world, that is, brings it together, synthesizes the many things he perceives and experiences, for the purpose of doing something with them. That something is to *bless them* to God, rather like a priest presenting a burnt offering to the Lord. A priest takes something ordinary and plain—say, a lamb—sees in it an expression of divine grace and man's condition, consecrates it to the Lord, and then commits it to Him by a specific act, at least part of which is *eucharist*, or thanksgiving. Then man *transforms* his life. He makes his ordinary experience in the world into something well-nigh sacramental, in which he observes the knowledge of God and the experience of God pressing in on him at every turn, in ways that elicit wonder, reverence, and delight. Increasingly, he responds with thanksgiving, praise, and a changed life, and actively seeks to increase in that knowledge and experience. His relationship with God, experienced in the ordinary events and things of everyday life, becomes more intimate, constant, and life-changing. As the creation speaks to him a word from its Maker and Sustainer, man responds by speaking back to God in thanks and praise, and by bringing his life more consistently into line with the revealed will of God. A conversational relationship grows between man as priest and God, and daily life becomes more sacramental and filled with the knowledge of God. The Scriptures tell us that God is revealing Himself to us in the things He has made (Ps. 19:1–6; Rom. 1:18–21). Created things are ambassadors of glory from God to His people. His "line has gone out" without words or speech in all the things that fill the firmament and the earth. As Schmemann puts it, "Each ounce of matter belongs to God and is to find in God its fulfillment . . . Nothing is 'neutral.' "[7]

William Cowper put it this way:

The Lord of all, himself through all diffused,
Sustains, and is the life of all that lives.
Nature is but a name for an effect,
Whose cause is God. He feeds the secret fire,
By which the mighty process is maintain'd,
Who sleeps not, is not weary; in whose sight
Slow circling ages are as transient days;
Whose work is without labor; whose designs
No flaw deforms, no difficulty thwarts;
And whose beneficence no charge exhausts.
Him blind antiquity profaned, not served,

With self-taught rites, and under various names,
Female and male, Pomona, Pales, Pan,
And Flora, and Vertumnus; peopling earth
With tutelary goddesses and gods,
That were not; and commending as they would
To each some province, garden, field, or grove.
But all are One. One spirit—His
Who wore the platted thorns with bleeding brows—
Rules universal nature. Not a flower
But shows some touch, in freckle, streak, or stain,
Of his unrivall'd pencil. He inspires
Their balmy odors, and imparts their hues,
And bathes their eyes with nectar, and includes,
In grains as countless as the seaside sands,
The forms with which he sprinkles all the earth.

—*The Task, 6.221–26*

We can already see, I think, that the task of theology involves much more than simply studying Scripture or reading academic tomes. We must discover some ways of interacting with God in the world. If we are truly to gain the benefit of theology—increasing knowledge of God—then we must be prepared to enter into a wider variety of activities through which God is revealing things about Himself and His purposes. We must, that is, prepare ourselves for doing theology and not just reading about it.

The Tools of Theology: Scripture and Sound Reason

Typically in the work of theology we depend on the tools of reason, deduction, logic, and verbal ability to produce a finished work of theology, in the form of either something written—a book or paper—or something spoken—a class lecture or sermon. As important—and necessary—as these tools are for this particular aspect of the theological task, however, they are by themselves insufficient for the task of knowing people and the world in which they live, as well as God, our Creator and Sustainer. Yet as we have seen, such studies are inextricably part of the work of theology. When we turn from the study of Scripture—which is the necessary foundation and constant touchstone for all our theologizing—to the study of creation, culture, and the actions of conscience, seeking from these what we may discover about God in order to raise our knowledge of Him to a higher level, we will need to develop new skills and master additional disciplines. We do not set reason, logic, and so forth aside, much less the Word of God. Rather, we supplement Scripture and reason with additional skills, tools, and disciplines that help us interpret the revelation of God that He is making through people and the world around us. We will shortly have somewhat more to say about these additional disciplines.

The Tools of Theology: Perceiving and Experiencing

Among the additional skills and tools that we must learn to use are what Frame calls "perceiving and experiencing":

> Perceiving and experiencing, then, are not activities sharply different from reasoning. They are processes by which we reach judgments, even if those judgments are not always correct . . . Data is presented to the senses. From that data, we infer the presence of objects or the existence of states of affairs.[8]

Perceiving and experiencing require us to engage our senses in interaction with other people and the world around us, so that by our senses—seeing, hearing, touching, and so forth—we may gather additional data that can help, in the light of Scripture, to enhance the knowledge of God that we seek.

How does that work, and why is it important? Let's begin with the latter question. Perceiving and experiencing are important because they allow us to come at truth from something other than a merely logical perspective. This is certainly not to say that reason and logic are not important, or not part of the process. Rather, by themselves, they are simply not enough for the task of doing theology by knowing people and the world so that we increase in the knowledge of God.

25

Perceiving and experiencing can supplement reason and logic in powerful ways.

1. *Enhancing understanding.* For example, it is one thing to say that a rose smells sweet. It is another thing altogether to smell a rose. The experience of that rich, sweet fragrance somehow greatly enhances our understanding of the adjective "sweet," as well as of the distinctive attributes of a rose. Or we may describe a mountain as so many feet high and so many miles long, or in such terms as "majestic," "immense," or "everlasting." To actually stand on that mountain, to climb it, or to look out from it to the valley below it makes those logical explanations and descriptions much more vivid, more thrilling and meaningful. We may define love in the strictest of biblical terms, elaborating its nature in careful and precise definitions and illustrations. But until we have experienced love for another human being—the selfless deed of kindness, the touch of a hand, the taste of a kiss—or observed love in action between human beings, our definitions must remain devoid of the vitality, warmth, and excitement that such experience can give them. Our intellectual comprehension of roses, mountains, and love—and of such associated ideas as beauty, majesty, wonder, and delight—is greatly enriched and becomes more meaningful as we perceive or experience these things that are the object of our intellectual activity, as opposed to merely reading or talking about them.

Experience and perception can thus work to enhance logical understanding, making it richer, fuller, and better able to serve the purpose of raising the level of the knowledge of God in us.

2. *Relating experience to intellect.* Reason and logic, at the same time, provide us with terms and categories to help us make sense of our experiences and to relate them to the whole of our knowledge. Once I have stood on or climbed a high mountain, I will have a greater appreciation of the meaning of the terms by which it or anything like it is described—awe, majesty, and so forth. And once I have gained, from my experience or perception of a mountain, a greater appreciation of such mountain-related ideas as immensity, majesty, beauty, awe, and power, I will be in a better position to associate those terms more meaningfully with the God who made the mountain when I read about Him in His Word. Experiencing and perceiving a mountain will make

my appreciation of it, and of its Creator, much deeper, richer, and more meaningful.

3. *Improving our walk with God.* Moreover, since the opportunity of perceiving and experiencing the people around us and the things of creation—as well as the God who reveals Himself therein—confronts us every moment of the day, actually doing so—doing theology by way of perceiving and experiencing in areas beyond Scripture or theological writing—can lead us to a more consistently self-conscious and richly rewarding walk with the Lord. We can expect doing theology like this to lead us to a deepening knowledge of God, more frequent prayer and praise, and more consistent transformation.

Emotions and Knowledge

In this respect, as Frame notes, "emotions contribute to knowledge" as well.[9] By feeling, for example, what people who are poor, oppressed, or dejected feel, our intellectual grasp of their condition is heightened, our sense of what God means when He says that He has compassion on the poor is enriched, and we are more likely to be moved to take some action in their behalf. In the same way, by allowing such emotions as fear, joy, awe, and wonder to be stimulated through activities of perceiving and experiencing, we strengthen our ability to feel those emotions in their proper relation to theological ideas, thus brightening and enriching those ideas in our minds, firming up our conviction about their truthfulness, and better preparing ourselves to act on them accordingly. We must not be run around by our emotions, perceptions, and experiences; rather, we wish them to "be placed in God's hands to be used according to His purposes."[10] This means that we have to bring our perceptions and experiences, as well as our emotions, back to the touchstone of Scripture and the doctrines that we, in dialogue with the church past and present, have determined to be the truth of God. Our perceptions and experiences, together with our emotions, may well shed more brilliant light on our logical understandings; doing theology can enhance reading theology. And these perceptions and experiences, in turn, will help to correct any faulty perceptions or emotions we may have experienced in our interactions with other people and with the world, and to discipline them for proper use in loving God and men.

The important point to emphasize, however, is that perceiving and experiencing people and the world around us—creation, culture, and the actions of conscience—can be a theologically and spiritually enriching activity. As we will see, this is what I mean by creational theology. Doing theology by attending to creation, culture, and the actions of conscience, through perceiving and experiencing, can deepen our knowledge of God. As James Sire notes, "Attending to reality is finally attending to God—the final reality and the author of all created reality."[11]

Theology as Discipline

I want to go back to Hoeksema's definition of dogmatics and pick up on one more idea that he mentions there. He writes, "Dogmatics is that theological discipline . . ." That's the word I want. Among the various activities to which the adjective "theological" may be applied, dogmatics is one. And dogmatics, like all other theological activities—including perceiving and experiencing—is a discipline. This implies three things.

The Need for Structure

First, all our work of theology must have some structure. Disciplines involve structure. We must set aside time and learn to employ specific skills and enter into specific activities that will allow us to achieve the end for which we are submitting to the discipline. In the work of theology—of knowing God—this means that we will need a certain amount of time to enter into the various disciplines of study, to dialogue with others, to engage in the perceiving and experiencing essential to theological studies, and to generate theological products of various kinds. This is what all theological study, if it is to be complete, requires. While we will make use of the disciplines of creational theology all along in our study, we will examine those disciplines rather more carefully in part 4.

28

Growing in the knowledge of God is the fruit of theological studies; therefore, we must determine that, somehow or other, we are going to find more time—or make better use of our existing time—in order to give ourselves to the activities required by this exciting and important calling. As part of this process, we are going to want to master those disciplines and skills of experiencing and perceiving that constitute the happy task of creational theology.

We must be careful here because our natural tendency when embarking on theological studies is to allocate all our time to reading, studying, exegeting Scripture, and comparing our findings with those of other theologians, past and present. This is important as the foundation for theology. But we must also make sure to reserve certain time for perceiving and experiencing—that is, for interacting via the senses with creation, culture, and people as they express the actions of their consciences—for what we can discover through these activities to enhance the knowledge of God. Proper discipline in theological studies will thus include a balance of activities—intellectual, perceptual, and experiential—engaging the mind and all the other senses as well in the disciplined pursuit of the knowledge of God.

Achieving an End: the Knowledge of God

Second, thinking of theology as a discipline means that we are attempting to achieve an end—the knowledge of God—that we desire to have an effect on us in the whole of our lives. It is not enough, in other words, for our theological studies merely to broaden or deepen the categories of our minds. The knowledge of God requires that we love Him with all our hearts, souls, and strength as well. Thus, we should expect not only our minds but also our affections and our daily conduct to be disciplined and shaped by our work in theology if the result of the knowledge of God is to be achieved. Knowing and loving God is expressed not only in the products of formal theological study—books, lectures, sermons, poems, conversations, and so forth—but in hearts devoted to God and lives rightly lived for Him. Those who truly know God offer up sacrifices of praise and thanks without ceasing, and show the effects of knowing Him in all their ways.

29

In other words, we will not have realized the benefit of theological studies, including our study of creational theology, unless, through growing in love for God and others, we are increasingly being transformed throughout, in every aspect of our lives, into the very image of Jesus Christ (2 Cor. 3:12–18). Unless we are beginning to think, feel, and act more like Jesus at every moment and in every situation of our lives, our theological disciplines will be faulty and our theology incomplete. We may have fallen into some imbalance between intellectual, perceptual, and experiential activities. Or one of these may be unduly dominating the others. Only as we achieve and maintain a proper balance in these areas, allowing the light that each receives to nurture the knowledge of God in us, will we grow to love Him more with all our hearts, souls, minds, and strength, and to love our neighbors as ourselves.

Of course, this implies that we have come to know Jesus Christ as the supreme manifestation of the glory of God, and as Savior and Lord of our lives (Heb. 1:1–3; John 14:6; Phil. 2:5–11; 2 Cor. 4:6). Knowing Christ—having entered into a saving relationship with Him by grace through faith—is the absolute starting point for all theological work. Jesus said that no one could come to the Father except through Him (John 14:6); therefore, in some sense at least, He must be the "gate" through which we pass in seeking to increase in knowledge of God. As Cowper advises:

> Acquaint thyself with God, if thou wouldst taste
> His works. Admitted once to his embrace,
> Thou shalt perceive that thou wast blind before:
> Thine eye shall be instructed; and thine heart,
> Made pure, shall relish with divine delight,
> Till then unfelt, what hands divine have wrought.
>
> —*The Task*, 5.779–85

We acquaint ourselves with God by believing in Jesus Christ for the forgiveness of our sins. Thus we enter into the true knowledge of God, which is then enhanced, and our lives are increasingly transformed, through the various disciplines of theological study, so that we grow

30

in the knowledge of God and our lives increasingly become a walk of worship and service in His name.

Theology an Ongoing Work

Finally, Hoeksema's definition invites us to consider that the discipline of theology is an ongoing work, one that will need to be adjusted from time to time in order for us to attain ever-greater levels of the knowledge of God. It is easy to fall into a rut in theology and devotional activities, or to allow them to become mere routines.[12] Yet if our activities of reading, study, perceiving, and experiencing are to serve as true disciplines in the calling and task of knowing God, we must be committed to them for the long haul, must exercise constant vigilance to prove their fruitfulness in our lives, and must be prepared to adjust them as necessary in order to ensure ongoing growth in the grace and knowledge of the Lord. In the work of theology proper we must learn how to exegete the Scriptures, compare and synthesize texts, analyze arguments and positions, and formulate theological conclusions. We must discipline our minds to undertake new tasks for the sake of knowing God. In other theological disciplines we must learn to engage our senses—grown dull by constant exposure to the noise of a secular age—to perceive and experience God's line as it goes out to us, for example, through the creation around us, and through people and their cultures. The more skilled we become at this discipline, and the more consistently we practice it, the more our knowledge of God will improve and our walk with Him be a daily conversation of joyful obedience, praise, and thanks.

It is the high calling and happy task of all who know the Lord Jesus Christ to press on in the disciplined pursuit of the knowledge of God, not merely for the sake of producing some theological product—a lecture, book, or sermon—but to increase love for Him and for our neighbors. This is the proper end of all theology, including the work of perceiving and experiencing—firsthand and by reading and study—which the disciplines of theological study demand.

Theology as Disciplines

From what we have seen thus far, allow me to suggest a definition of theology as the disciplined pursuit of the knowledge of God. In doing theology we are setting aside time for reading, studying, reflecting, thinking, perceiving, and experiencing with the single-minded objective of knowing God—of growing in love for Him with all our hearts, souls, minds, and strength. These activities will find us engaged with Scripture as the starting point and touchstone of all we do. But they will also find us dialoguing with others—past and present—and actively attending to the revelation of God in creation, culture, and the actions of conscience. As a result of this work of doing theology, we hope to grow in grace, both within, in our spirits or inner persons, and without, in our practice of the Christian faith. We improve both our assurance of salvation and our ability to love our neighbors as ourselves (Heb. 11:1). Theology as the disciplined pursuit of the knowledge of God is potentially the most rewarding activity in which any human being can invest his or her time and energies.

Windows on God's Self-Revelation

But as we saw earlier, doing theology involves understanding and beginning to master a wider range of fields than simply Scripture and theological writings, and a broader array of skills than just reading, thinking, and writing or teaching. Doing theology requires that we enter into every arena where God is pleased to reveal Himself, seeking diligently and carefully—by perceiving and experiencing—whatever light He may be shining upon us, and comparing what we find in each arena in order to build up a better understanding of God and grow in love for Him.

In my study, where I am writing these words, two windows afford me a vista on the reality without. Each of them offers only a partial view of what is going on outside. From where I sit, if I look out the westernmost window only, I can see the four pine trees bordering my yard, my neighbor's driveway, the home across the street to the northwest and the street itself, the boxwood bush in front of my window, and a small portion of my yard. I might be tempted to think that this is the whole of outside reality, and spend many hours observing what goes on out there, thinking about how all these things and activities relate to one another, pondering their significance, and perhaps writing a poem or essay about them. Undoubtedly there are unlimited ways that I could describe what I see just beyond the westernmost window in my study.

But another window at the east end of my study also lets in light from the reality outside, and it affords me a totally different vista. As I look out this window from the same vantage point, I see my in-laws' home to the northeast across the same street (a most happy sight, I hasten to add), my own driveway and the Japanese maples that border it, my neighbor's home directly across from me, the yard, more boxwoods, the mailbox, and so on. Something in me wants to connect these vistas—perhaps along the road or by means of the yard—and paint a larger picture for my imagination of the real world beyond my windows. If I had more windows, I could see the oaks in my front yard, the front walk, the sky above my neighbors' homes, more of the road, and so on. The more windows I add to my study, the more vistas—and different vistas—I will gain on reality without, and the better will be my understanding of the world beyond my study, and, perhaps, of my place in it.

Just so God has provided us with six different and wondrous windows through which He is revealing Himself and His glory for our inspection. They are truly windows of glory. Each is a particular discipline of theological studies, through which God reveals Himself and His purposes by different means and in different lights. By learning how to observe Him through each of these windows—how to *do* theology and so get at God's revelation through the skills germane to each discipline—we can expect that our understanding of God and His purposes will grow, and we will realize more fully the end of theological studies, which is the knowledge of God.

The Disciplines of Theological Studies

Because my purpose in this book is to concentrate primarily on just one of these windows of glory—that of creational theology—at this point I will only mention these six windows of theological studies:

- Biblical theology
- Creational theology
- Historical theology
- Systematic theology
- Spiritual theology
- Practical theology

Like true windows, each of these areas of study affords a different look at the whole of revealed reality, opening up on a particular vista of God and His ways, purposes, and truth, and letting in a certain kind of light. Each area of study is composed of a number of subdisciplines that help us to do theology more effectively and comprehensively. By applying ourselves through the disciplines of reading, study, perceiving, and experiencing to each of these areas of theological studies, according to the nature and demands of each, we can expect to grow in the knowledge of God. Through the disciplines of theological studies—including creational theology—our love for God and our neighbors will be consistently enriched. As one of the windows of glory, creational theology places unique demands on our attention, the nature of which it is the burden of this book to explore.

The Inescapability of Theology

Let us admit that the work of doing theology like this may appear a daunting task. For many of us, just finding time to read and study the Scriptures with any degree of faithfulness is difficult enough. Thinking about learning how to use additional disciplines, such as those involved in creational theology, and actually making use of them with any regularity, is perhaps more than we can imagine ourselves doing. For some it might seem better to leave theology to the theologians. But there are three reasons why this is inadvisable.

Theology Is Inescapable

First, none of us can escape the work of doing theology. We are made in the image and likeness of God (Gen. 1:26–28); God has put eternity in our hearts, a sense of transcendence that keeps us yearning to know Him (Eccl. 3:11). This explains why there has never been a society without some form of religion, and why the presence of religion and spirituality remains so strong in a secular age such as ours. People simply cannot do without God; something in them compels them to seek Him out. If they will not pursue knowing the God of Scripture, then they will fabricate gods of their own and devote themselves to them (Rom. 1:18–32). If, as Grenz and Olson suggest, theology at its most basic level "is any thinking, reflecting or contemplating on the reality of God—even on the question of God,"[13] then it is clear that theology is alive and thriving in our day. Whether that theology is healthy and true is a different question.

God's Revelation Is Inescapable

Second, just as we cannot escape the inward urge to pursue theological truth, given that we are made in the image of God, we cannot escape the revelation of God. God is "pouring forth" information about Himself day and night, all the time (Ps. 19:1–6). People see that information, and it serves to reinforce in them the knowledge of God with which they are naturally endowed (Rom. 1:18–21). Granted, not everyone admits to seeing God through the things He has made, but this act of denial and suppression of the knowledge of God does not free them from theological activity. Instead, as Paul points out (Rom. 1:21–32), and as we will examine more fully later on, it simply sets them on a course of *bad* theology, leading to sin and death. It seems that those who will not have recourse to the revelation of God in the ways that He gives it will do their own theological work as best they can and according to their personal interests and needs. Which means that they will do theology poorly.

Given that God is working so hard to make Himself known, it would seem important for us to discover and make use of the various disciplines He has provided for us by which we may penetrate that revelation unto a truer and more beneficial knowledge of God.

Doing Theology Is Inescapable

Finally, and because of the two reasons already mentioned, we cannot escape doing theology; the only question is whether we will do it poorly or well. If we ignore the resources that God has given us for knowing Him, or content ourselves with only one or two of them, how can we expect to do anything other than incomplete theology at best? How can we hope to be always improving our knowledge of God, and growing in love for Him and our neighbor, if we never choose to look through more than one or two of His windows of glory, or if we look through those windows improperly, merely casually or occasionally, or without sufficient skill to observe all that is revealed through them? Or if we simply ignore a window, such as that of creational theology? As Grenz and Olson observe, "the difference between lay theologians and professional theologians is one of degree, not kind."[14] Both can do good theological work; however, both can do poor theological work as well. In order to do good theological work, both lay and professional theologians will have to give themselves more diligently and completely to the task of seeking the knowledge of God in all the places and by all the means in which He is pleased to reveal Himself.

God Is Inescapable

We cannot get away from the task of theology because we cannot get away from God. He impresses Himself upon us continually, calling us to know and worship Him, and He will not be denied. Whether we know Him really and truly, and learn the joy of pursuing Him with all our hearts, souls, minds, and strength, depends on the diligence and care with which we take up the challenge of doing theology, observing God through all the windows of glory where He is making Himself known.

The Inevitability of Theology

Theology, as we have seen, is an inescapably human task. It is also therefore inevitable. Because we are made in God's image and hunger

36

for transcendent reality, and because God is always revealing Himself to us in unmistakable ways, human beings will think theologically in the present, whether or not they diligently apply themselves to the task. The human mind is always active, taking in and processing the information around it, trying to determine what that information teaches about God (or "god"). Our affections will also always be stimulated one way or another with respect to theology. Like the mind, the heart will be busy—even if only at a kind of subconscious level—nurturing affections to draw or repel us in one way or another with respect to God and His purposes. Our consciences will also be engaged in the task of theology, either growing and improving in the ability to function according to the works of the law of God (Rom. 2:14–15) or hardening and encrusting with wicked works, becoming laws unto themselves (Heb. 10:22). And our lives will reflect the extent to which theology—whether good or bad—has molded and shaped us in the inner person. That is, human beings cannot help but practice theology—whether they practice it poorly or well. All our practices—our habits, routines, manners, and so forth—are informed by our theology. Since what comes out in our words and deeds is the product of what we think and feel, and since our hearts, minds, and consciences are inescapably and inevitably theologically active, our practices cannot be otherwise.

Christians must be concerned, therefore, that the theology that informs their minds, affects their hearts, shapes their consciences, and comes out in their lives is the best and truest it can possibly be. This will mean more time and attention devoted to the disciplined pursuit of the knowledge of God through the windows of glory where He is revealing Himself to us, including the window of creational theology.

The theology in which we become involved in this life provides but a foretaste of the life to which God is delivering us in glory, as we will see. It is, however, a *true* taste, and well worth learning to savor. Believers in Jesus Christ are bound for an eternal day when basking in the glorious radiance of unimpeded, unhindered theology is their great privilege and joy. In that day we will know our God fully, face to face, even as we are known (1 Cor. 13:12). For the time being, we have the great privilege, as followers of Christ, of preparing for that great day and of living in the there and then, here and now, by devoting ourselves to the happy task of theology—pursuing the knowledge of God through the windows of glory.

And in that wondrous array of disciplines, the happy task of creational theology can open up vistas on God's general revelation that can lead us to greater wonder, reverence, delight, and transformation in our walk with the living God.

Questions for Study or Discussion

1. Reflect on the term *theology*. What thoughts and feelings does that term arouse in you? Why?

2. Would you be content for your pastor to be a poor or mediocre theologian? Or to be indifferent to theology? Why or why not?

3. How would you assess your own progress in "knowing God" to date? Are you satisfied with where you are in your relationship with Him? Could doing theology better and more consistently enhance your knowledge of God? In what ways?

4. How do you respond to the idea of "perceiving and experiencing" as part of the theological task? Have you ever done theology like this?

5. What goals would you like to set for your study of creational theology? How would you like to see yourself grow in your relationship with God as a result of this study? What kinds of things would tell you, after finishing this study, that it was worth your while?

The Happy Task of Creational Theology

Activity 1

Purchase a small notebook that you can carry around with you all the time. It should be small enough to fit in a pocket or purse—perhaps a small spiral-bound notebook will do. I use part of my daily planner, which I have with me at all times. Use this notebook to begin making observations from creation, culture, and the actions of people's consciences. Here's how to begin doing this.

- Pay attention to things around you—the beauty in the creation, the wonders of cultural artifacts (music, machines, fashion, etc.), and the ways in which people express what's going on within them, in their souls (consciences). Do this as part of your normal daily routines, or set aside some time to go for a walk, sit on your porch, or walk through a mall.
- Let your curiosity and feelings lead you to observe things carefully. Write down your observations, whatever strikes you as standing out amid the routines of your daily activities, suggesting the presence of wonder, beauty, majesty, goodness, or some other aspect of God's truth. Make just a few brief notes to record your perceptions and experiences. What did you see? Why did this catch your eye? How did you feel about it?
- Spend time thinking about your observation. Mull it over in your mind. Do any passages of Scripture come to mind, or any biblical truths suggest themselves? At some point, add these reflections to your notes.
- Before going any further in your study of creational theology, get your notebook and get started. Do the following:

1. Make at least one entry in your notebook, following the outline above. Your final entry—after you have observed, reflected, added biblical insight, and perhaps record a few other thoughts—should take up about one page in a small notebook (no larger than 3″ x 5″).

2. Find someone to talk to about your observations. Tell that person—who will become your "conversation partner" for this study—why you are doing this and what you hope to gain from it. Ask your friend to pray for you as you go through this study and begin taking up the happy task of creational theology. Agree to meet together occasionally so that you can share what you are learning, as well as what you are perceiving and experiencing, concerning the work of creational theology.

PART 2

GENERAL REVELATION AND CREATIONAL THEOLOGY

An Unseen Energy
"He sends out His command to the earth . . ."
(Ps. 147:15)

An unseen energy pervades the air
this crisp, still winter morn, sustaining all
that is. The barren, sleeping trees stand tall
because of it; the day breaks bright and fair,
responding to its ancient power. The ground
holds firm, and oxygen in just the right
amount swirls in my lungs. The gathering light
of day reveals the splendor all around
me that, but for this presence everywhere,
would dissipate, dissolve, desist, and be
no more. No ear can hear, no eye can see
this fearful, gracious presence, but it's there.
  The heart of faith alone can recognize
  what otherwise escapes both ears and eyes.

2

General Revelation (1): An Overview

*The heavens declare the glory of God;
and the firmament sheweth his handywork.*
—Psalm 19:1

*Our natural understanding and the works of cre-
ation and providence so clearly show God's goodness, wisdom, and power that human beings have no
excuse for not believing in Him. However, these
means alone cannot provide that knowledge of God
and of His will which is necessary for salvation.*
—Westminster Confession of Faith, 1.1[1]

Pied Beauty

Glory be to God for dappled things—
    For skies of couple-colour as a brinded cow;
      For rose-moles all in stipple upon trout that swim;
Fresh-firecoal chestnut-falls; finches' wings;
    Landscape plotted and pieced—fold, fallow, and plough;
      And all trades, their gear and tackle and trim.

43

All things counter, original, spare, strange;
   Whatever is fickle, freckled (who knows how?)
   With swift, slow; sweet, sour; adazzle, dim;
He fathers-forth whose beauty is past change:
   Praise him.

                —*Gerard Manley Hopkins*

A Revelation of God in Creation and Providence

From the earliest days of the church, theologians have commented, mostly in passing, on the revelation of God in the things He has made. The opening words of the Westminster Confession of Faith, quoted above, nicely summarize the understanding of the great thinkers of the church from virtually all ages: There is a revelation of God in the works of creation and providence. That revelation clearly testifies of God's wisdom, goodness, and power. The revelation of God in creation and providence is in fact so clear that human beings cannot ignore it, and should be led by it to acknowledge His existence, to seek Him out, and to put their trust in Him. Yet for some reason (which the Confession will later explain) they fail to do so; the revelation of God in creation and providence is not sufficient to reveal the way to the true knowledge of God. For that, and for man's salvation, more and different light from on high is required.

Thus the Westminster divines raise in our minds the same questions to which Hopkins provoked us in the introduction to this volume. What is that revelation? Why can some discern it while others generally ignore it? What use is to be made of this revelation? If it does not lead us to salvation, then what does God intend by making Himself so clearly known in the things He has made and sustains? And in light of the preceding chapter, we might further inquire, What is the place of this revelation from God in creation and providence in the work of doing theology? In growing in the knowledge of God?

The theologians and pastors who met in London from 1643 to 1648 were not merely compiling the accumulated wisdom of the church on what is known as the doctrine of general revelation. Instead, they were seeking to summarize a theme of Scripture that recurs consistently throughout its pages. In this chapter I want to briefly examine that theme and then to consider how theologians in the Reformed tradition have developed it for their peculiar purposes. We will see that in all the dappled, stippled, spare, and strange things that God has made, as well as in the artifacts of culture and the activities of human conscience—all their trades, tackle, and gear—there is much to be observed of the grandeur of God as He "fathers-forth" therein, and many reasons and ways to bring praise to His glorious name by learning to see Him there.

The Biblical Doctrine of General Revelation

A complete treatment of the biblical doctrine of general revelation is beyond the scope of this present study. In chapter 3 we will look at more of the biblical evidence and guidance for understanding this doctrine. For now, we will examine only two of the *loci classici* of this biblical teaching. These will suffice both to justify the claims of the Westminster divines and to encourage us in our quest for more light on this important subject.

General Revelation according to Psalm 19:1–4

The first text is Psalm 19:1–4:

The heavens declare the glory of God;
And the firmament sheweth his handywork.
Day unto day uttereth speech,
And night unto night sheweth knowledge.
There is no speech nor language,
Where their voice is not heard.
Their line is gone out through all the earth,
And their words to the end of the world.

From this text we may draw four conclusions.

1. First, there is, indeed, a revelation of God in the things of creation, a manifestation of His glory bearing testimony to His exis-

tence, wisdom, and power—to His glory. That revelation is far off, coming at us from the highest reaches of space; yet it is also right at hand, in the very air we breathe. It is real revelation; that is, it bears true messages about God, messages from which we should expect to be able to learn about Him and His purposes, truth, and ways.

2. Second, the psalmist wants us to understand that this revelation is both profuse and constant. God veritably floods the creation with manifestations of His glory, and He does so in all its parts, day and night, and in every culture and among all peoples. God is always revealing Himself through the things He has made; the whole world flames out and oozes and fathers-forth His glory and grandeur at all times. Creation is, indeed, a capacious reservoir of means for knowing God.

3. Third, that revelation is clear and unmistakable. While it uses no words or speech, yet there is no mistaking the fact that God is declaring Himself to the world. What is revealed is not just a manifestation of beauty or a provocation to awe. It is God Himself, His presence, making Himself known, and beckoning us to reflect on Him, His purposes, His truth, and His ways.

4. His revelation is, in the fourth place, ubiquitous. God's glory is inescapable, unavoidable. It goes out through all the earth and is heard to the end of the world. No one can hide from its light or avoid the proclamation it makes of the reality and glory of God. As we saw in our last chapter, God and His revelation are inescapable. So too are our responses to Him.

We must face up to the realization that, daily and in every place, we are confronted with the fact of God's revelation of Himself and His glory in the things He has made. We have it on the authority of His Word, and we are left with the same questions as before: If God is so profuse, so constant, so clear, and so unavoidable in revealing His glory in the things He has made, why do so few seem to take notice and respond accordingly? And what use should we who *can* perceive that glory make of what He is telling us of Himself and His purposes? And how can we come to perceive that glory more clearly?

God's Revelation according to Romans 1:18–23

The answer to these questions is provided, at least in part, by our second passage, Romans 1:18–23:

> For the wrath of God is revealed from heaven against all ungodliness and unrighteousness of men, who hold the truth in unrighteousness; because that which may be known of God is manifest in them; for God hath shewed it unto them. For the invisible things of him from the creation of the world are clearly seen, being understood by the things that are made, even his eternal power and Godhead; so that they are without excuse: Because that, when they knew God, they glorified him not as God, neither were thankful; but became vain in their imaginations, and their foolish heart was darkened. Professing themselves to be wise, they became fools, and changed the glory of the uncorruptible God into an image made like to corruptible man, and to birds, and four-footed beasts, and creeping things.

Here Paul can be seen to be reiterating what the psalmist declared: God has plainly revealed Himself in the things He has made, so clearly that all people actually possess a knowledge of Him, and know something of His power and divinity. But Paul adds two further observations that should urge us onward in our desire to learn how to make proper use of the revelation of God in creation.

Ungrateful people deny God's general revelation. First, Paul observes that ungrateful men deny the revelation of God in creation and providence, although it is plainly evident to them. They turn for meaning, comfort, and security to the worship of created things. Though they think they are wise in ignoring God's self-revelation in creation, and strenuously occupy themselves with the things of their own hands, they are actually fools. William Cowper saw this plainly:

> Man views it, and admires; but rests content
> With what he views. The landscape has his praise,
> But not its Author. Unconcern'd who form'd

47

The Paradise he sees, he finds it such,
And such well pleased to find it, asks no more.

—*The Task, 5.791–95*

Men may deny the reality of God, proclaiming themselves atheists, but this does not negate the fact that, according to Scripture, they truly do know Him, at least at some level. In this respect many people are like alcoholics. They are in the thrall of a factual reality that they refuse to admit and, by refusing, allow themselves to persist in self-destructive patterns of behavior, even in the face of indisputable facts. Still the revelation of God presses upon them—"nature is never spent" in declaring God's glory, as Hopkins reminded us in "God's Grandeur." Ungrateful men, however, have a way of dealing with this: they bury the knowledge of God in unrighteous thoughts, words, and deeds as they continue on their merry way, ignoring what God is pleased to show them of Himself, and worshiping all the more fervently their peculiar idols.

Ungrateful people fall under the wrath of God. Second, Paul tells us that as a result, ungrateful men become the objects of God's wrath, which He is even now revealing from heaven in judgment of their foolish ways. This takes the form, as Paul goes on to say in verses 24–32, of God's gradually but continually giving them up to greater degrees of sin and blindness, until they make ruin of their lives and go to their graves as condemned men who will perish forever before the judgment seat of God. Paul could almost be seen to be thinking that if only ungrateful, idolatrous men could be made aware of their great offense against God, and of how He responds to their ingratitude, they might be brought to their senses, made fearful of God's wrath, and led to cry, like the people in the streets of Jerusalem on the day of Pentecost, "Men and brethren, what shall we do?" (Acts 2:37).

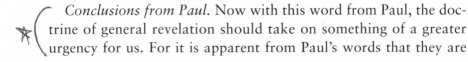

Conclusions from Paul. Now with this word from Paul, the doctrine of general revelation should take on something of a greater urgency for us. For it is apparent from Paul's words that they are foolish and ungrateful who do not take the time to observe what God is revealing of Himself in the creation, to acknowledge with thanks His glory, and to consider what use they ought to make of this revelation in worshiping and serving Him. And they come under His judgment as a result, and can expect something less than the full and abundant life promised by our Savior so long as they continue to tread the earth unmindful of the grandeur of God on display all around them.

Further, Paul makes no distinctions among men in this passage; he does not say, "Of course, the *redeemed* are exempt from any proper acknowledgment of God's glory in the things He has made, and though they may consistently fail to praise Him for His revelation in creation and providence, they need not expect Him to treat them with disfavor." Rather, Paul wants us to believe that anyone and everyone who takes for granted, ignores, or denies the glory and grandeur of God in the things He has made is, at least in some measure, outside the will of God and in danger of coming under His rod of discipline.

These two passages are representative of many, many other places in Scripture where the doctrine of general revelation is set forth. They show us that God is truly and clearly revealing things about Himself, His glory, His purposes, and His ways in the things He has made. He expects people to take note of Him there and to respond to Him with thanks and praise, and to order their lives accordingly. And His patience is taxed by those who disregard or fail to make proper use of the revelation He is clearly, continuously, and profusely communicating in the things of creation.

Reformed Theology and General Revelation

Reformed theologians, beginning with Calvin, have not failed to take note of the general revelation of God, and to offer advice as to what use God intends for it. Again, this is not the place for an exhaustive study of the teaching of our theological forebears. Instead, a brief summary will have to suffice.

John Calvin on General Revelation

We begin with Calvin, who in many of his works reveals a deep appreciation of the ways in which God is making Himself and His glory known through the things He has made. In the *Institutes* Calvin wrote:

> Lest anyone, then, be excluded from access to happiness, [God] not only sowed in men's minds that seed of religion of which we have spoken but revealed himself and daily discloses himself in the whole workmanship of the universe. As a consequence, men cannot open their eyes without being compelled to see him. Indeed, his essence is incomprehensible; hence his divineness far escapes all human perception. But upon his individual works he has engraved unmistakable marks of his glory, so clear and so prominent that even unlettered and stupid folk cannot plead the excuse of ignorance.[2]

Here Calvin elaborates on what we have previously seen when he says that there is something that inheres in the very fact of our humanness—he calls it a "seed of religion"—that itself bears testimony to the existence of God, an argument that he develops in chapter 2 of Book 1. The image of God in which men are created bears unmistakable, unerasable testimony to the existence of God. This, coupled with the revelation of God in creation, makes the knowledge of God inescapable.

Calvin continues by showing that the works of human culture not only help us in discerning the revelation of God in creation, but can themselves accomplish God's revelatory purposes as well:

> There are innumerable evidences both in heaven and on earth that declare [God's] wonderful wisdom; not only those more recondite matters for the closer observation of which astronomy, medicine, and all natural science are intended, but also those which thrust themselves upon the sight of even the most untutored and ignorant persons, so that they cannot open their eyes without being compelled to witness them. Indeed, men who have either quaffed or even tasted the liberal arts penetrate with their aid far more deeply into the secrets of the divine wisdom. Yet ignorance of them prevents no one from seeing more than

enough of God's workmanship in his creation to lead him to break forth in admiration of the Artificer.[3]

The liberal arts, Calvin suggests, can help us to look more deeply into the things of creation, and enable us to discern more clearly what God is revealing of Himself. But while they can be helpful, they are not necessary for anyone to see "enough of God's workmanship" in the creation around to be led to give Him praise and thanks. His revelation is sufficiently plain for all to see evidence of Him in the works of creation and providence.

Yet people do not:

> Here, however, the foul ungratefulness of men is disclosed. They have within themselves a workshop graced with God's unnumbered works and, at the same time, a storehouse overflowing with inestimable riches. They ought, then, to break forth into praises of him but are actually puffed up and swollen with all the more pride. They feel in many wonderful ways that God works in them; they are also taught, by the very use of these things, what a great variety of gifts they possess from his liberality. They are compelled to know—whether they will or not—that these are the signs of divinity; yet they conceal them within. Indeed, there is no need to go outside themselves, provided they do not, by claiming for themselves what has been given them from heaven, bury in the earth that which enlightens their minds to see God clearly.[4]

As Paul observed, the practice of sinful people is to deny or ignore the revelation of God that He is making in them, the creation, and the things of human culture, and to claim for themselves all that they see. Meanwhile, they "bury in the earth"—in their sinful thoughts and practices—the knowledge of God and any sense that He is revealing Himself to them by the things He has made.

Calvin's thought on the subject of general revelation can thus be seen to be consistent with that of the Scriptures, although he develops it somewhat with a view to the implications and applications of this doctrine for his own place and time.

Abraham Kuyper on General Revelation

We have already briefly noted the comments of the Westminster divines on general revelation. We move on to Abraham Kuyper, the great nineteenth-century theologian and statesman. Kuyper shows the close affinity of the doctrine of general revelation with other doctrines—such as common grace, natural law, and natural theology—in the thinking of Calvinist and other Christian theologians:

> A Calvinist who seeks God, does not for a moment think of limiting himself to theology and contemplation, leaving the other sciences, as of a lower character, in the hands of unbelievers; but on the contrary, looking upon it as his task to know God in *all* his works, he is conscious of having been called to fathom with all the energy of his intellect, things *terrestrial* as well as things *celestial*; to open to view both the order of creation, and the "common grace" of the God he adores, in nature and its wondrous character, in the production of human industry, in the life of mankind, in sociology and in the history of the human race.[5]

Kuyper is much more insistent than Calvin that revelation from God can be discerned in the created order as well as in the works of human culture and the actions of men's consciences. These "terrestrial" things have much to say about God, and part of the believer's "task" is to discover the knowledge of God in all His works. Kuyper devoted his entire life to this task, making notable contributions to the knowledge of God not only in works of theology but also in journalism, education, public policy, and statesmanship.

Elsewhere Kuyper wrote of the relationship between these "celestial" and "terrestrial" studies. He insisted on the necessity of each for a full and proper knowledge of God. But he also argued that what he called the "spiritual sciences"—theology proper and its related disciplines—must be the basis on which we attempt to understand the revelation of God in the things of creation, which can be discerned through the "exact sciences":

> It is not as if the *essence* of the object of the spiritual sciences contains deeper mysteries (for with the exact sciences, the essence is equally mys-

terious), but knowledge of the relations of the object of these sciences is so difficult to obtain because these relations are so uncertain in their manifestation and are almost always bound to the self-communication of the object.[6]

The "object" that is providing "self-communication," which both the spiritual and exact sciences are able to discern, is God. Kuyper says that it is difficult to relate our observations from these two areas. He continues:

Again and again it appears that there are all sorts of spiritual things which we know with far greater certainty than the facts which are brought to us by the observation of things seen. We nevertheless cease to be a man when the reality of spiritual things is not more certain to us than what by investigation we know of plants and animals. We maim our science when we deny it access to spiritual objects.[7]

God has been pleased to make truth about Himself more readily obtainable through the spiritual sciences—the study of Scripture and the work of speculative theology. Yet the exact sciences are also telling us something about God, and we cannot discover what they are disclosing unless we bring to bear on those studies the certainties that we have concluded in our work in the spiritual sciences. Kuyper concludes:

There is no other course therefore, than to construct the spiritual sciences from the subject itself; provided we do not overlook that the subject of science is not this inquirer or that, but *the* human consciousness in general. The two sciences differ, in that the element of the visible world enters into our consciousness by a different way than the element of the spiritual world. The elements of the visible world work upon our powers of representation through the senses, while in entire independence of our senses and of any middle link known to us, the elements of the spiritual world affect our subject spiritually, and thus to our apprehension appear to enter immediately into our consciousness.[8]

How does the mind reconcile its discoveries in the spiritual and exact sciences—in special and general revelation, we might say? We look to

53

our spiritually informed minds, which are being enlightened by Scripture and theology, to guide us in the work we do through observing, listening, sensing, analyzing—as well as perceiving and experiencing—the revelation of God in creation. The spiritual light we receive through the spiritual sciences must be allowed to serve as the guide by which we pursue the task of seeking the light that God is revealing to us through the exact sciences. This is perhaps what the psalmist had in mind when he wrote that "in thy light we shall see light" (Ps. 36:9).

Kuyper offers a considerable advance in understanding the doctrine of general revelation from what we saw in Calvin or the Westminster divines, although the seeds of his thought can certainly be discerned in those forebears.

G. C. Berkouwer on General Revelation

Twentieth-century Reformed theologian G. C. Berkouwer has provided a lengthy and very helpful treatment of this subject in his book *General Revelation*. While his primary purpose is to refute Barthian claims that there is no such thing as a revelation of God in creation—since, according to Karl Barth, Christ alone is God's revelation and all else is but a witness to Him—Berkouwer affirms the conclusions of previous Reformed theologians and urges us on in the task of seeking the knowledge of God in creation. Concerning the fact that some men, such as Hopkins, Cowper, Calvin, Kuyper, and many others, are able to acquire insight into the glory of God in creation, Berkouwer wrote:

> This harmony and this outlook, this *insight*, can only be thus explained that man *in* and *by* the salvation of God is *delivered* from the tenacity of the egocentric and commences to sing *to the glory of God*. It is this salvation that opens doors and windows toward God's handiwork, and God's majesty above heaven and earth is beside, and immediately connected with, the *horn*, which God has exalted for his people (Ps. 148:13, 14). Here nature is no longer separated from and dissolved from her creatureliness and not elevated to an idol, but known—as creature—with the stamp of her Maker.[9]

Now we're getting somewhere! Berkouwer tells us, in agreement with Kuyper, that only those who have come into the light of saving grace are able to discern the revelation of God in creation and common grace. What's more, this is part of God's "horn"—His summons—to His people, that they should seek out the knowledge of Him in this realm. But how do we do this?

> The thing which is needed here is *eyes* which are able to see and discover. And there are those that seeing, do not *see* . . . This understanding, and seeing, and hearing, is possible only in the communion with him, in the enlightening of the eyes by the salvation of God, and by the Word of the Lord. But this seeing and hearing is *not* a *projection* of the believing subject, but an actual *finding*, and *seeing*, and *hearing!* Here nothing is "read into," but it is only an *understanding* of the *reality* of revelation.[10]

We need to develop eyes to see, ears to hear, and senses to experience— all in the light of God's revelation in Scripture—what our Creator and Sustainer is telling us about Himself, His purposes, and His ways through the things He has made. And we need to be convinced that this is *real* revelation, not just the reporting of perceptions or the recording of highly subjective impressions, and that it can enrich and deepen our experience of the Lord and, presumably, our service to Him in this world.

Reformed theology, thus, is mainly clear in its affirmations concerning the reality of general revelation, its purpose, and its importance in the divine economy.[11] And while Reformed thinkers have made suggestions about how to approach general revelation in a manner consistent with its divine purposes, as well as what use to make of it, we still seem to be in need of some more concrete examples of how to proceed. This we will find, among other places, in the creational theology of Jonathan Edwards, which we will examine in part 3.

Problems with the Doctrine of General Revelation

Given that the Scriptures seem so clear about the matter of revelation from God through the things He has made, and that the community of Reformed theologians (among other Christian thinkers) has so consistently and emphatically underlined the validity of this area of study, we might wonder why so little actual work seems to be proceeding in this area. How can it be that so few books, seminars, and workshops exist to train our thinking and to equip us to make best use of the doctrine of general revelation? Why is it that hardly any people within the Christian community, whether lay or clergy, give much thought to or undertake much practice in this area at all? Why does our disciplined pursuit of the knowledge of God not involve more of the work of what I am calling creational theology? Why does the glory of God discerned in the things of creation not feature larger in our Christian education, worship, and everyday conversation? Why are there so few products of creational theology—books, art, poetry, music, lively conversation, and so forth—in evidence among Christians today?

Explanations for the relative paucity of work in the area of general revelation and creational theology lie somewhere along a spectrum of extremes that we can identify as expressing problems with the doctrine of general revelation. Between the rocky shores of the maximizers of this doctrine and the imposing cliffs of its minimizers, the ship of the church drifts aimlessly on a vast ocean of uncertainty, fearing to beach on either shore, and unable to identify a safe harbor within which to put down anchor.

The Maximizers of General Revelation

Maximizers of the doctrine of general revelation fall into two categories. These thinkers tend to make more of the doctrine of general revelation than can be justified from the teaching of Scripture.

1. Some maximizers, for example, will say that general revelation is so true and reliable an expression of God as to be virtually identified with Him. In this category we might include a variety of pantheists—animists, ecological extremists, a whole host of New Age sects, and even some who can be found within segments of mainline Christian churches (such as the Gaia-worshipers). In the view of such people, certain aspects of the creation (if not all of it) are coextensive with

God and are to be regarded and revered as such. Evangelical and Reformed Christians, rightly wary of this group of maximizers, do not wish to become identified with them, and so steer a course away from their generally pantheistic teachings and claims.

2. A second group of maximizers can be found more solidly within the household of faith. These are the advocates of natural religion and natural theology who maintain—if I may float a very crude caricature—that the revelation of God in Scripture is clear and compelling, and can actually lead a person to the true knowledge of God, if not to salvation. In certain Roman Catholic and classical evangelical apologetics, varieties of natural theology—arguments from design, teleological and ontological arguments, and so forth—are employed to clear the beach of resistance and prepare a landing place for the gospel. Proponents of this view of general revelation tend to believe that they can argue a compelling case for the existence of the God of the Bible from appeals to nature, history, science, logic, the human conscience, or other areas of general revelation unaided by Scripture. Only after such work has been done, they suggest, should we land the assault force of the gospel, rather like docking a precious vessel in a well-prepared slip. That is, only when our work in natural theology has established agreement over the existence, or at least the *probable* existence, of the God of the Bible should we unfurl the banner of Scripture and the good news of Christ. In the process of "preparing the way" for this unfurling, reference to Scripture is generally avoided; all mention of such theologically loaded terms as "sin" and "propitiation" is carefully steered away from; and every attempt is made to establish "bridges" of consensus and consent between the unbeliever and his worldview and the apologist and his aims. General revelation, this view maintains, is sufficient to create an assent to the idea of God—which the apologist wrongly assumes will be the God of the Bible, but see Romans 1:20–25—on the basis of which a case for the gospel may then be successfully argued.

Certain Reformed thinkers have advocated this view, and many Reformed Christians accept it at least implicitly. And no want of energy and effort has been expended in this direction over the past two generations. Yet for all the many admirable and earnest labors in this area, the beaches of our postmodern world are more firmly entrenched with enemy machine guns and artillery than ever before. And the landing crafts of eager evangelists are still tied up alongside the troop carriers, waiting for the beaches to be cleared by what they regard as the heavy artillery of evidentialist apologetics. In spite of two generations of such apologetics, however, the island of the world seems more firmly in the hands of the enemy than ever, and the vast majority of believers, called to be witnesses for Christ, are still cowering in the assault vessels of the pews.

The Minimizers of General Revelation

Minimizers of the doctrine of general revelation also fall into two classes.

1. The first of these insists that there does not, in fact, exist anything like the general revelation concerning which we have been speaking, either because God has revealed Himself exclusively in His Son (the Barthian view) or because sinful people are so hardened and blind that they cannot perceive anything He might want to say (certain Reformed thinkers of the early twentieth century). Among those influenced by such thought we would expect to find no interest in developing the doctrine of general revelation or the practice of creational theology, and learning to use these to our advantage in the kingdom of God.

2. The second group of minimizers probably encompasses most of us from the evangelical and Reformed communities. These minimizers tend to see general revelation as real and undeniable; but they view it as an imposing height, scalable only by special forces and inaccessible to the rest of us. General revelation is true and reliable. It really does manifest the glory of God and speak to us about His purposes and ways. But getting on top of what is revealed there is not the ken of ordinary folk, or even most pastors. A very few scientists, one or two artists, and a handful of abstract philosophers and historians are making some progress up the slope, hollering back down to us—in books and seminars—concerning the amazing discoveries they are making en route. We are fascinated and encouraged, but because we have not seen these things for ourselves and know that we are not

really qualified to scale that height and make best use of them, we simply leave them alone and occupy ourselves with other concerns. The rich seams, verdant valleys, lush forests, and glorious peaks of general revelation, lying just beyond those imposing heights, remain for us something to admire from afar, mostly at second hand, and only as objects of fascination and wonder.

Yet Reformed pastors, church officers, and lay men and women continue to confess the teachings of the Westminster Confession of Faith, even as they decline to take up the disciplines necessary for making proper use of the revelation of God coming to us through the capacious reservoir of creation, culture, and the actions of the human conscience.

Conclusions

From what we have briefly considered, the following conclusions are inescapable.

1. *There is revelation from God in creation.* The Bible insists on it, as does virtually the whole of the Reformed tradition: there is revelation from God in the things He has made. He is speaking to us in the creation, through the elements of culture, and in the actions of human consciences expressed in practices of various kinds. The unseen energy of divine providence courses through the whole of divine creation, pouring forth speech about our sovereign God. Since God is speaking, therefore, ought we not to be listening, trying to discern His word through creation, and discovering how it can help to further our knowledge of God and improve our love for Him and our neighbors?

2. *We are accountable for that revelation.* God is not pleased for us to ignore Him whenever, wherever, and by whatever means He is speaking to us. His wrath—or His chastening and discipline—comes on those who simply turn away from His revelation in the creation because it is too difficult to understand, susceptible to various interpretations, or simply inconvenient. We must learn to cultivate the eyes of faith that will allow us to perceive and experience God in creation, so that we may be good stewards of His revelation there. "As creatures made in God's likeness, this is at once our privilege and our task. There is

59

joy out there in the creation of our God. As image bearers, it is our holy vocation to notice it, love it, revel in it, and preserve it."[12]

3. *It is possible to "hear" God through general revelation.* Disciplines exist for us to use in gaining access to the knowledge of God in creation. Just as we must learn to read and reason in order to hear Him speaking in His Word, so we must learn to perceive and experience Him as He pours forth speech about Himself in the world around us. We would not think of trying to excuse ourselves from the hard work of reading and learning how to interpret Scripture. We must nurture the same attitude when it comes to the revelation of God in creation. The disciplines of creational theology, while they will involve the eyes and ears, will teach us how to nurture the eyes of faith, so that we can see into what would otherwise escape our notice.

4. *General revelation is a vital source of spiritual growth and vitality.* Any revelation of God, gladly received and properly understood and embraced, can reveal His glory and proceed with us along the path of sanctification and transformation. It is worth whatever sacrifices we must make for us to be able to meet God as He is revealing Himself in creation, culture, and the human conscience. For in so meeting Him we will grow to love Him more, and find more power for loving our neighbors as ourselves.

But in order to make use of general revelation through the disciplines of creational theology, we must first turn to the Scriptures in order to learn how we must approach this aspect of the theological task. For the Scriptures are the greater light of God within which we will be able to make sense of the lesser light coming to us through general revelation.

Questions for Study or Discussion

1. Had you been familiar with the doctrine of general revelation before reading this chapter? What is your understanding of what God reveals to us there? Have you ever experienced any sense of encountering God through general revelation?

2. If sinful people cannot—or will not—see the revelation of God in creation, culture, and the ways of men, then what good is that revelation? Do you think we should be appealing to this kind of revelation to help others think about Him? Why or why not?

3. Do any areas of general revelation—the created world, human cultures, or human relations and history—appeal to you? Which? Why? Is it realistic to expect that you might discover God revealing Himself in these arenas?

4. How might you expect to benefit from being able to discern the revelation of God in creation, culture, and the ways of men? What dangers lie along this path?

5. Can you expect to know full and abundant life in Christ if you willfully ignore His revelation of Himself in Scripture? Why or why not? What about His revelation of Himself in creation?

The Happy Task of Creational Theology

Activity 2

By now you have made several entries in your notebook, observations of creation, culture, and the actions of conscience that have caught your attention and made you wonder what they might be saying to you of God, His purposes, His truth, or His ways. Set aside some time before you read the next chapter to do the following:

- Meditate on your observations. Try to relive your experience of seeing and recording them for the first time. Add some more notes about what it was that initially struck you as you wrote your observations down for the first time.
- Ask yourself: What in particular about God, His purposes, His truth, or His ways does this observation bring to mind? Does it make me think of any particular Scriptures or biblical truths? Prayerfully meditate on these questions, and make some additional notes in your notebook.

61

- Now ask yourself: How does this observation help to brighten or enliven the biblical texts or truths that have come to mind as a result? Make some further notes.
- Close this time of meditation in prayer, talking with the Lord about your observations, meditations, and preliminary conclusions. Continue making additional observations day by day in your notebook.
- Get together with your conversation partner and share your observations from this activity.

3

GENERAL REVELATION (2): TWO CAVEATS, FACETS, AND GOALS

The works of the LORD are great,
sought out of all them that have pleasure therein.
—Psalm 111:2

Creation is a book proclaiming the Creator. It is a
book of beauty that our intellect reads, but through
the passageways of our five senses.
—Thomas Dubay[1]

The Booke of the World

Of this faire Volumne which wee World doe name,
If wee the sheetes and leaves could turne with care,
Of Him who it correctes, and did it frame,
Wee cleare might read the Art and Wisedome rare?
Finde out his Power which wildest Pow'rs doth tame,
His Providence extending everie-where,

His justice which proud Rebels doeth not spare,
In everie Page, no, Period of the same:
But sillie wee (like foolish Children) rest
Well pleas'd with colour'd Velame, Leaves of Gold,
Faire dangling Ribbones, leaving what is best,
On the great Writers sense ne'er taking hold;
Or if by chance our Mindes doe muse on ought,
It is some Picture on the Margine wrought.

—*William Drummond (1585–1649)*[2]

The memorable closing scene of the film *Grand Canyon* finds the principal members of the cast, all of whom have known turmoil, confusion, and disappointment in life, staring out in silent wonder at the vast expanse of the Grand Canyon. A welcome sense of peace and well-being settles on them—and on the audience—as they are lifted somehow above their petty squabbles, mundane concerns, and paltry fears and doubts into an experience of transcendence that they do not understand but cannot deny. We are happy for them, and for the peace they have found. They and we are caught up in an ecstasy of greatness, wonder, and majesty that seems to say, "Look up, look beyond, look to things that last, and that shimmer with unspeakable beauty, goodness, and power, and know peace." We leave them there, and yet we come away from the experience saying, "Yeah, that's what it's all about."

For an all-too-fleeting moment, they and we have come face to face with a glory and grandeur that we can neither deny nor explain, and it has taken our breath away. Through the power of cinema, a wonder of creation has arrested our attention, and every true believer has no difficulty coming away from that experience convinced that the characters in *Grand Canyon*, and the audience too, have had an encounter with the living God. We have witnessed a kind of manifestation of God, or some revelation concerning His ways, in one of the lavishly illustrated pages of the book of the world and the response of those who resorted there for peace, mediated through the wonders of contemporary technology. God has shown us something of Himself and His ways through creation, culture, and the actions of human conscience.

We have had an experience of God's general revelation in what we have perceived. What we do with that revelation can have huge consequences for our lives. The task of creational theology is to help us read the pages of the book of the world so that we might "finde out his Power which wildest Pow'rs doth tame / His Providence extending everie-where."

In this chapter we want to examine in somewhat more detail the biblical teaching about the subject of general revelation, which we introduced, defined, and traced historically in the previous chapter. Our purpose here is to further develop a foundation for explaining the role of creational theology in helping us to respond to God's general revelation as He intends, so that His purposes in so revealing Himself may be realized. We will look first of all at two caveats that must be kept in mind at all times whenever we take up the work of creational theology. Next we will consider two facets of God's general revelation that are consistently treated throughout the pages of Scripture. Finally, we observe two goals that God has set for the revelation of Himself in the things He has made. In our next chapter we will begin to consider more carefully how the work of creational theology can help us to make proper use of God's general revelation in working to realize those purposes.

Two Caveats

Before we get too far into our study of the principles and goals of general revelation, or the ways in which creational theology can help us to realize God's purposes in giving that revelation, we need to set forth two caveats that must guide us at all times in this work.

God Is Ultimately Inscrutable

"O the depth of the riches both of the wisdom and knowledge of God! How unsearchable are his judgments, and his ways past finding out!" (Rom. 11:33). Because God is who He is, and we are but finite, fallen creatures, at best only partially restored in soul and body, we must be content not to expect our study of general revelation and our

65

practice of creational theology to yield anything akin to an exhaustive or final insight into the matters God reveals there. We must always remember, as Alister McGrath reminds us, that "the human ability to discern God within the natural order is arguably fragile at the best of times."[3] At the same time, we do expect to learn something of God and His purposes, truth, and ways from His revelation in creation, culture, and the actions of conscience. As McGrath comments, "We are authorized by Scripture to seek a partial disclosure of the glory of God through the works of God in creation."[4] We can expect to gain further clarification of biblical teaching, more potent experiences of God's truth, means for better communicating our faith, and guidance in how to respond to the God who thus reveals Himself. But we cannot move from general revelation to statements of finality about the nature and purposes of God. Our studies in general revelation will not even yield as much intellectual or theological certainty about such matters as our study of Scripture. But this should not lead us to conclude that such studies are unimportant, or that they cannot aid our study of Scripture in significant ways.

Therefore, we must always take up the work of creational theology in dialogue with and submission to the work of biblical and systematic theology, as well as all the other windows of glory through which it pleases the Lord to reveal Himself. We must allow our study of Scripture, in other words, to provide the guiding principles and theological categories for our work of creational theology, for only the words of Jesus, received under the tutelage of the Holy Spirit, give us the life and understanding we need in order to make sense of His works (John 6:63). As McGrath puts it:

> If nature is to reveal the Christian God, it must be regarded as creation—
> that is, as bearing some relation to God, in order that this God may
> somehow be disclosed through it. Natural theology cannot become a
> totally autonomous discipline, independent of revelation, in that it
> depends for its credibility upon the revealed insight that God is the cre-
> ator of the natural order.[5]

66

So we must always let our observations of general revelation, and any conclusions regarding God's revelation there, be tempered and guided by our study of Scripture. God, who is ultimately inscrutable, has made Himself more clearly known in the "greater" light of biblical revelation. While the "lesser" light of general revelation yields true and reliable knowledge of God, that knowledge can be fully appreciated and rightly used only in the light of God's fuller disclosure of Himself in Scripture (Ps. 36:9).

Our Reason Is Always Fallible

The works of the inscrutable God in creation, culture, and the human conscience are so many and so complex that no one individual, nor all great minds together, can comprehend them. His ways are, indeed, past finding out: "Many, O LORD my God, are thy wonderful works which thou hast done, and thy thoughts which are to us-ward: they cannot be reckoned up in order unto thee: if I would declare and speak of them, they are more than can be numbered" (Ps. 40:5). In his comment on Genesis 1:1, Chrysostom teaches us the appropriate humility with which to approach the practice of creational theology:

> Let us accept what is said with much gratitude, not overstepping the proper limit nor busying ourselves with matters beyond us. This is the besetting weakness of enemies of the truth, wishing as they do to assign every matter to their own reasoning and lacking the realization that it is beyond the capacity of human nature to plumb God's creation.[6]

What is true for all theological work is true for that of creational theology as well: many heads are better than one. Proper use of creational theology requires an ongoing dialogue with thinkers, perceivers, and creators from many disciplines, present and past, whose insights and observations can enrich our own, and help us steer clear of the rocks of shallow thinking. We cannot do this work as theologians alone. Nor can artists, scientists, or sociologists hope to contribute to this field without entering into and sustaining a dialogue with a wide assortment of those whose labors bring them into the arena of creational theology, particularly those who share our faith in Jesus Christ. Richard Mouw writes of this high calling:

> Discernment is, of course, a key requirement. We need the Spirit's guidance in our hearts and minds as we seek to identify traces of the Spirit's work in the larger creation. And we need to ground ourselves in the life and thought of that community where the Spirit is openly at work, regenerating sinners and sanctifying their inner selves.[7]

And even when our discussions and research have ranged far and wide, and we are prepared to offer some conclusion from our work in creational theology, it must always be made somewhat tentatively, inviting comment and response from others who are also engaged in this important work.

But again, this should not be taken as minimizing the work of creational theology. General revelation and the creational theology that helps us to interpret and use it are important, both to God and to human beings. We must make of it what we can; yet we must make good and wise use of it, and try by every means to avoid frivolous, specious, or presumptuous investigations and conclusions. Keeping these two caveats in mind at all times can help to create a better yield from our labors in this field.

Two Facets

Two facets to general revelation demand that we take more than a merely passive interest in this aspect of God's self-disclosure. First, there is the fact that God calls us to consider His works; then there is the question of what we may expect to learn of Him there.

God Calls Us to Consider His Works

First, the Scriptures are clear that part of what God intends for us as creatures made in His image is that we should consider His works, should make careful study of them in order to see His hand at work in the creation. The "great Writer" intends that we should "take hold" of Him as He has revealed Himself in the book of the world. As Scott Hoezee puts it, "For this whole world belongs to God—we should want to know more about it."[8] While this is an underlying thought in many places in Scripture, it is plain and undeniable in at least six places, each of which we will examine in brief.

1. *Romans 1:18–21*. We have perhaps already said enough about this passage. Yet I simply want to reiterate what is implicit there, namely, that God has invested Himself in the things He has made, is revealing Himself there, and is not pleased when people do not acknowledge His revelation and give Him thanks and praise. The created things of the world clearly show the deity and power of God; all people see this revelation from God, and will be held accountable for what they have done with it. Those who shrug it off, suppress it, or simply ignore it will find that His wrath begins to be revealed against them. Those who acknowledge God's revelation in the creation can expect to experience His favor and to prosper in knowing Him and His ways.

2. *Psalm 111:2*. This is the passage that opens this chapter. Those who do take the time to consider the works of the Lord will delight in them, and will be encouraged to look more closely into them for what they can reveal to us of our God. The operative word here, *derushim*, "sought out," has a variety of meanings, including "study," "resort to," "frequent," "read repeatedly," "discuss," and "inquire" or "investigate." While not all these meanings apply in this place, these various nuances help to flesh out for us what the psalmist intends here: God's works are worthy of our diligent, careful, thoughtful, and eager attention. We must "turne with care" the "sheetes and leaves" of the book of the world. The more we attend to them, the greater will be our delight in them, and the more we will make the time to consider them even further.

3. *Ecclesiastes 1:13*. This is not easy work, however, even though it's what we're made for: "I resolved to inquire and investigate, as wisely as I could, everything that has been done under the heavens. This is a difficult matter which God has given to the children of humankind to busy and afflict them."[9] The task to which Solomon devoted himself, a portion of which he reports on in Ecclesiastes, is a task given to all

human beings. We are called to investigate everything that has been created according to the divine purposes and plans—the meaning of "under the heavens." It is important to note this phrase. It's not enough simply to learn about art, or study science, or be an astute "people-watcher." Lots of people are already doing that "under the sun," that is, from a strictly naturalistic and secular perspective. The challenge to the followers of Christ is to try to understand things as God does, to "think God's thoughts after Him," concerning every aspect of the creation. This is a "difficult matter." It can almost seem an affliction, since it takes time, requires learning new skills and disciplines, and demands great patience of all who enter into it. We may not pursue it, to borrow a phrase from Jonathan Edwards, "by the bye," looking only at some "Picture on the Margine" of the book of the world. Instead, we must devote ourselves to this task, difficult and demanding though it may be. We cannot all study and learn everything; yet we must each take up a portion of this difficult but happy task.

4. *Proverbs 25:2.* "It is the glory of God to conceal a thing: but the honour of kings is to search out a matter." While only a king may have had leisure to take up this work in Solomon's day, all the "royal priesthood" of God, who are the followers of Jesus Christ (1 Peter 2:9–10), are now called to this happy task. God's glory is "concealed" in the things He has made; it is the glory (same word) of God's vice-rulers (cf. Ps. 8) to "search out" (here, *chaqor*, "search through, explore, examine thoroughly") whatever matter is before them, to discover the glory of God "concealed" there. So while this work of examining everything that God has made, with a view to discerning His self-disclosure and purposes, can be a difficult task, the reward of encountering the glory of God in creation is worth the effort, and brings the kind of enjoyment in perceiving and experiencing, and delighting in the Lord, that spurs us on to more such investigative efforts. This has certainly been my own experience in doing the work of creational theology.

5. *Psalm 46:8–11.* "Come, behold the works of the LORD, what desolations he hath made in the earth. He maketh wars to cease unto the end of the earth; he breaketh the bow, and cutteth the spear in sunder; he burneth the chariot in the fire. Be still, and know that I am God: I will be exalted among the heathen, I will be exalted in the earth. The

LORD of hosts is with us; the God of Jacob is our refuge." There is practical benefit to be realized from considering the works of God through the actions of human conscience—in this case, wars. The powers of nations, and all their fury toward one another, are in the hands of God. He disposes them as He will, and calls His people, in the midst of international conflagrations, to quiet their hearts and seek His presence amid the frenzy and fury of warfare. In the midst of vast international struggles—as in all the actions of conscience—we may discern the presence of God. As we do, we are able to be at peace, and to rest in the strong hands of Him who is our refuge and shelter. He is, indeed, our Mighty Fortress.

6. *Matthew 6:28.* "Consider the lilies of the field, how they grow." In a similar vein, our Lord Jesus commanded us to consider the creation for what we may learn from it about the ways of God with people—His providential care. Not only here but also in His parables Jesus resorted to general revelation as a platform from which to proclaim profound truths about His kingdom. Mustard seeds, farmers working in fields, men laboring in business, objects of great price and value, armies marching to war, builders erecting towers and barns: all these—aspects of the creation, matters of culture, and issues of the conscience—and many more served as powerful vehicles of revelation in the hands of Him who used them to teach us about that kingdom into which He has, by His grace, translated us (Col. 1:13). If our Lord could see so much in the creation to encourage and instruct us, is it not reasonable to expect that we should be able to do the same, if only we will take the time to "consider the lilies"?

It is clear that God expects His people to take up the work of creational theology, those disciplines that enable them to discern Him in His general revelation, so that they might discover His glory there and grow in grace and truth. While we do not expect to see everything as clearly as God does (Eccl. 3:11), we may expect to see His glory and grandeur flaming and oozing out of this capacious reservoir of revelation that is His creation, the book of the world. To ignore this calling is to deny a significant aspect of God's redemptive purposes. In Jesus Christ, God is reconciling all things back to Himself (Col. 1:13–20), and He has called us into this ministry of reconciliation as

His ambassadors (2 Cor. 5:19). How can we possibly hope to make progress in this important aspect of our redemption if we remain willfully indifferent to the revelation of God in the things He has made, and refuse to take up the work of creational theology in obedience to His Word?

God Expects Us to Learn from His Works

Our examinations and considerations of God's revelation of Himself in creation, culture, and the actions of conscience can yield insights into the nature of God and His purposes, truth, and ways. Indeed, we might go so far as to say that our studies and investigations in *any* of these areas—in any of the "chapters" of the book of the world—remain incomplete until they have led us to some conclusions about the God who created and sustains all things. We do not expect what we learn here to differ from what we find out through the study of Scripture; rather, we will come to see biblical truth more clearly, in something of a better light, and with our minds better informed and our affections more fully engaged as a result of considering the revelation of God in the things He has made. We expect the revelation of Scripture, in other words, to be confirmed and augmented by our studies in general revelation, using the disciplines of creational theology.

We also expect, through seeing God's hand in all that He has made, to improve our stewardship over the creation in all its aspects, to make use of it in ways more consistent with what we see Him doing, and not just for our own shortsighted and selfish ends. As we see the care, beauty, and consistency with which God expresses Himself in the works of His hands, we will be led to imitate His ways in our own use of the creation.

In particular, God expects our studies in the book of the world to help us grow in two ways—in the knowledge of God and in the understanding of His purposes, truth, and ways.

Improving knowledge of God. It is important to remember that in the book of the world, God is revealing Himself. He is making Himself and His glory known, and in such a way that we might learn of

72

Him through what He is revealing. We expect to find our understanding of God heightened, our delight in Him enriched, and our love for Him greatly strengthened as He reveals Himself to us through creation, culture, and the actions of conscience. Through the practice of creational theology we can expect to gain new insights into the nature of the Godhead itself, together with a better appreciation of the great power by which He subsists and upholds all things (Rom. 1:20). We will be led to reflect on that power and to experience it more intimately as we contemplate the soothing waters of a calm lake or the raging waves of an ocean storm, the might and devastation of an earthquake, the thunderous brilliance of a nearby lightning strike, the coming of fall, or the birth of a living thing (Ps. 29). We will understand better what the Scriptures mean when they speak of the splendor and majesty of God as we experience these things in some work of His hands, such as the Grand Canyon. Perceiving and experiencing splendor and majesty before such a wonder, we will be better able to recall that experience, and the affections associated with it, when the Scriptures describe God in such terms (Ps. 111:3).

Some act of kindness observed by one person toward another may touch us with the graciousness and compassion of our God (Ps. 111:4). His power perceived and experienced, say, in a mighty storm, or in the bringing down of some tyrant, may encourage us to lay hold of that power in taking the gospel to all nations (Ps. 111:6; Acts 1:8). The heavens and earth exist and continue by the power of His Word, which He has commissioned us to proclaim to all the nations, and to believe that as surely as it accomplishes His purposes in divine providence, it will do so in the work of redemption (Ps. 147:15–20; Isa. 48:12–13; 55:11).

Observing the works of God in the things He has made, we get a better sense of the many and varied ways in which He cares for us day by day (Matt. 6:25–34), most of which we simply take for granted. We are reminded that He is faithful and good, and steadfast in His love for us, as He continuously attends to our every need, just as He does the lilies of the field and the birds of the air.

All these observations, made amid the wonders and works of God's creation, impress us more deeply with the truths of what we read about

73

God in His Word. We find our hearts more fully engaged with ideas of beauty, goodness, greatness, majesty, justice, splendor, might, and lovingkindness. We find our affections stirred, so that we are better able to experience what it feels like to know and love this God, as our affections are disciplined according to His purposes, truth, and ways. We are arrested by the constancy of His presence and care. We understand Him better and take greater delight in knowing Him. And we find our love for Him, and awe in His presence, increasing and growing stronger. Surely this is a result to be cherished and diligently pursued!

Improving understanding of God's purposes, truth, and ways. We also expect our studies in God's general revelation to give us better understanding of His purposes, truth, and ways—the "Art and Wisedome rare" by which He governs all things, His "Providence extending everie-where," and "His justice which proud Rebels doeth not spare."

Job concluded from his observations of beasts and birds and other aspects of creation that true counsel comes from God, not from officious friends full of pop psychology; that even the highest judges can act foolishly and the mighty be overthrown; and that great nations rise and fall at the pleasure of God (Job 12:7–25). God Himself was able to lead Job to humility and repentance—God's purpose for men before Him—by a tour de force of the creation, as He reminded Job of His great power and unsearchable wisdom to be observed there (Job 38–41). Jesus pointed to a prodigal child, a late-arriving bridegroom, and a master seeking an accounting from his stewards to instruct His followers about what God is like and how we must relate to Him. In these vignettes He also implied much about how we are to make use of those aspects of creation entrusted to our care, whether they be money or possessions, people or lands, or opportunities and responsibilities. By perceiving and experiencing what God does in and through His works, we can learn what He expects of us, and thus improve our stewardship over all that He has made, and our calling as His followers to reconcile all things back to Him.

God expects us to take the time to observe His glory in the things He has made, and to learn both how to know and love Him better and to discern and live more consistently according to His purposes and ways. Scott Hoezee writes that

> a major part of our Christian vocation should be the nurturing of delight in this universe of wonders—a delight similar to God's own playful joy in creation, which we see traced for us in Scripture. This world teems with opportunities for such delight—the question is whether we take the time to notice.[10]

Most Christians expect to gain this knowledge exclusively through the study of Scripture—"colour'd Velame, Leaves of Gold, / Faire dangling Ribbones"—while "leaving what is best"—God's revelation in the creation—unexamined or, if examined at all, only "by chance." These things ought not to be. As Alister McGrath insists, "the Christian understanding of the ontology of creation demands a faithful investigation of nature."[11] Creational theology provides the tools and guidelines for this happy task.

Two Goals

Whenever God reveals Himself, He has goals in mind; He intends to accomplish something. From the teaching of Scripture we may discern two goals for God's self-revelation in the things He has made. In fact, these are no different from goals He has established for His revelation in Scripture: to increase and improve worship of God, and to advance the work of sanctification. Taking a creational-theology approach to general revelation, according to the will of God, helps us to realize these divine goals more completely.

Increase and Improve Worship of God

God will be worshiped. He alone is worthy of worship. And in worshiping God human beings—indeed, all of creation—find their highest fulfillment and delight (Ps. 96). One of God's goals in revealing Himself through creation, culture, and conscience is to help us in worshiping Him as is His due. General revelation can increase and improve our worship, but only if we learn from what God is revealing about Himself in creation, culture, and the actions of conscience through the disciplines and tools of creational theology.

God reveals Himself through the things He has made in order to aid our worship of Him in three ways.

The expression of worship. General revelation is designed to aid us in the ways in which we express our worship to God. Through it, for example, God intends to draw out from His subjects expressions of thanksgiving in worship (Rom. 1:18–21). Those who observe God's revelation in creation, culture, and the actions of conscience, and fail to respond in expressions of gratitude for what they discover there, are in danger of turning away from God to idols, and thus coming under His wrath. The revelation of God in His works—His majesty, splendor, power, and so forth—provides plenty of grist for thanksgiving, if only we will learn to observe Him in the things He has made.

God's revelation of Himself in His works can also enrich the vocabulary of praise that His faithful people offer up to Him. The psalms are rich in suggestions of where we might look to see the hand of God at work. Let's consider just one example: Psalm 104. God's handiwork—and hence His glory—is visible in the landscapes of mountains and seas (vv. 5–9); the daily course of streams and rivers (vv. 10–13); the proliferation of plants and animals, and their habits and habitats (vv. 14–18); the regularity of seasons and days (vv. 19–20); the vocations of men (vv. 22–24, 26); the seas and everything in them (vv. 25–26); the provision of the needs of all creatures (vv. 21, 27–28); the cycles of death and life (vv. 29–31). God Himself rejoices in all His works and the glory they reveal (v. 31); we His people should do the same, with just the kind of specificity indicated here and elsewhere (v. 33).

Many Christians today are suffering from an impoverishment of language with which to praise God. So many of the praises we hear—whether offered in groups or sung with the lyrics of contemporary "praise songs"—sound too much like, "Lord, we really just praise You," and not enough like what we read in Psalm 104. By paying more attention to the details of the glory of God revealed in His works, we can greatly improve the language with which we come before Him to offer our praise and thanks. God is pleased with such worship; indeed, it is one of the reasons that He has both revealed Himself in creation, culture, and the actions of conscience and taken the time in His Word to point these things out to us. We can expect to know God more personally in worship as we improve our vocabulary of praise, for as the psalmist reminds us, it pleases God to inhabit the praises of His people, especially when those praises are offered according to His own guidelines and words (Ps. 22:3).

God also gives us His revelation in the things He has made in order to improve our offerings to Him. Conscious of the Lord's ownership of all He has made, various psalmists offer back to Him in worship certain aspects of general revelation that they intend as acts of devotion, such as time (Ps. 90:12); work (Ps. 90:16–17); bodily members (Ps. 141:3, 8); affections of various kinds (Ps. 141:4); relationships (Ps. 144:12); even adversaries and trials (Ps. 21:8–13). Such offerings might also include the products of creational theology—conversations, works of art, poems, songs, and much more. The act of offering these things to the Lord establishes a commitment that leads in practice to an entirely different approach to the use one makes of such things day in and day out, and to the increase of such things to the glory of God. But this can happen only when such things as these—and many more— are acknowledged as coming from God, as revelations of His glory, and therefore as rightly in need of being devoted back to Him (cf. 1 Cor. 4:1–7).

Finally, if we recognize that God can be glorified in works of culture, we may be more motivated to create and support the creation of new forms devoted to promoting worship of God. Hence the many exhortations to sing a new song to the Lord (cf. Ps. 98:1). It seems clear to me that a poem such as the one that opens this chapter, an artifact of culture, reveals something about God and His ways and has great power to encourage the knowledge of God, which leads to worship. Who will deny that certain musical compositions—for example, J. S. Bach's church cantatas and oratorios—can do the same? Even paintings, sculptures, films, stories, and all kinds of popular arts and crafts[12] can be means of worship and can provoke us to worship, for we see the hand of God and the revelation of His truth in them. So can

77

lively group discussions and sweet conversations with family and friends. If we understood that God uses such artifacts of culture to reveal something about Himself in order to aid us in worshiping Him, we might as a community be more enthusiastic about supporting those who have a calling from God to labor in these arenas to His glory.

In all these ways, and doubtless more, God intends that His revelation of Himself in the works of His hands should aid us in expressing our worship of Him.

The experience of worship. Similarly, God is revealing Himself in the things He has made to help us improve our experience of worship. Observing God's glory in general revelation can help us grow in the fear of God (Ps. 111:7–10), that deep-seated reverence and awe of His holiness and might that reminds us of the wrath He is capable of exercising against sinners, and keeps us diligent in praising and thanking Him and pursuing holiness in the Lord. General revelation can lead us to a more vibrant and sustaining sense of hope. In Job 14 the sufferer is reflecting on the troubles that fill human life, and wonders whether man has any reason to hope (1–6). Yet the annual renewal of trees leads him to believe that even though all men must die, a day is coming when they will be renewed to life, without all the trials of the present (vv. 7–12). Job, looking past his present suffering to that great redemptive future, inspired by his observation of the trees, longs for God's winter to engulf him so that he might know His springtime sooner rather than later (vv. 13–15).

Seeing the revelation of God in the things He has made can also increase our joy in worshiping God (Ps. 92:4). As we learn to see God's work in creation, culture, and the actions of conscience, we will be led to exult and be glad in Him, to triumphantly boast of His sovereign goodness, beauty, and truth.

As a worshiper of God and a leader of worship, I often realize that our experience of worship frequently lacks much in the way of real fear, hope, or joy. These affections, when engaged, cannot help but affect our bodily disposition—in smiles or tears, shamed faces cupped in palms, hands spontaneously thrust heavenward, eyes lifted above, falling to our knees, or shouting in joy—all the kinds of expressions of worship that we see throughout the psalms, but that are all too often missing from contemporary (especially Reformed) worship. God has been pleased to reveal Himself in the things He has made precisely to aid us in knowing Him and experiencing these and other affections more deeply as we come before Him in worship.

⌐ *The extension of worship.* God is pleased to reveal Himself in general revelation to aid in the extension of our worship, helping us both to increase time in public worship and to take worship beyond the times of public gathering and make it more a part of our daily and moment-by-moment experience of the Lord.

It stands to reason that if our worship vocabulary is augmented and our experience of worship intensified, our time together in worship as the people of God will increase. People do what they delight to do. At present, it pleases us to worship God according to culturally prescribed time parameters occupying Sunday morning for about an hour. Go beyond that, and people begin looking at their watches. There are other things that it pleases them to do. But when our worship, informed during the rest of the week by our observations of God's glory in the things He has made, becomes richer with thanks, praise, and offerings; when it is enhanced by the addition of new songs to the Lord; and when in worship we know more intimately and intensely the fear, hope, and joy of the Lord, we will not resent the extra time that our morning worship is extended to accommodate our pleasure in worshiping God. And we will return to worship Him on Sunday evenings, and perhaps midweek, or even at other times. Like most other things, improvement and increased pleasure in worship lead to increased time in worship, helping to fulfill one of God's goals for pouring forth speech about Himself, manifesting His glory to us day by day in the things He has made.

Further, as we become accustomed to seeing God's grandeur flame out and ooze around us throughout the day, we will be more given to wonder, praise, thanksgiving, testimony, and worship as part of our daily course. Worship will increasingly become a way of life, so that our minds are constantly alert to the presence of God and our hearts continuously responsive to Him. This can lead to sweet moments of silent meditation, brief interruptions of prayer and praise, lively lunchtime conversations with fellow worshipers, and even set-aside times to retire from daily business to meet with the Lord for prayer.

God is revealing Himself in the things He has made in order to encourage us to worship Him more and worship Him better. Using the disciplines of creational theology to discern the revelation of God in creation, culture, and the actions of conscience can help us to realize this divinely established goal.

Advance the Work of Sanctification

"And the very God of peace sanctify you wholly . . ." (1 Thess. 5:23). It is the will of God that His people should grow in the grace and knowledge of our Lord and Savior, Jesus Christ (2 Peter 3:18). He calls us to press on in the work of "perfecting holiness in the fear of God" (2 Cor. 7:1), and He has given us His Word and Spirit as the primary means to realize this objective (John 17:17; 2 Cor. 3:12–18). Yet it stands to reason that wherever God is revealing Himself, His goal in so doing must be consistent with the revelation He has given in His Word. Therefore, we may reasonably conclude that He intends the revelation He is making of Himself in creation, culture, and the actions of conscience to aid and encourage us in our sanctification. General revelation is a means of grace, and it can help us in working out our salvation in fear and trembling (Phil. 2:12–13). It can do this in three ways: by providing a check against sin, by encouraging us in holiness, and by enhancing our witness.

Providing a check against sin. Let us remember what Paul says about general revelation: those who fail to submit to God's purpose in so revealing Himself—to give Him thanks and praise—turn instead to idols for their worship outlet, and spin off into a life of sin and rebellion against the Lord, incurring His wrath (Rom. 1:18–32). If ignoring or neglecting or even suppressing the revelation of God in creation, culture, and conscience can lead to sin, is it not reasonable to assume that observing that revelation, and responding with improved worship, can provide a check against sin? If we are daily more and more

80

conscious of the presence of the Lord around us, and enthralled with the revelation of His glory and grandeur, we will be less inclined to follow those paths that we know to be displeasing to Him. If my moments each day are more and more being filled with spoken and unspoken words of adoration, praise, and wonder, my mind and heart will not be inclined to consider paths offensive to the Lord, the awareness of whom increasingly fills my days with holy delight. Practicing the disciplines of creational theology can thus aid us in realizing God's purpose for making Himself known through general revelation, that we, being ever mindful of Him, might fear and love Him, and guard against the inroads of sin.

Encouraging the pursuit of holiness. This seems to be the conclusion to be drawn from Job 42:1–6. Throughout the course of Job's trials, his relationship with God was in danger of compromise. Though he began his first trial well, accepting the necessity of suffering and declaring his resolve to trust in the Lord even though He should slay him (Job 2:10; 13:15), as his suffering progressed and his "friends" became more insufferable, Job persuaded himself that God owed him an explanation for all that had befallen him. In chapter 31 we find him veritably demanding of God an accounting for His actions against him:

> Oh that one would hear me! behold, my desire is, that the Almighty would answer me, and that mine adversary had written a book. Surely I would take it upon my shoulder, and bind it as a crown to me. I would declare unto him the number of my steps; as a prince would I go near unto him. (Job 31:35–37)

Yet even at this outburst, God remains silent. Only after Elihu has added his insights to the conversation does the Lord speak and sort things out. And when He does, it is not as analyst or preacher or counselor that He comes. In chapters 38 to 41 all God does is to take Job on a grand tour of creation, pointing out the wonders of the created world and reminding him that He who created and takes care of all this is also the one who watches over His servants, even when they are suffering. At the end of God's impressive rebuke, Job replies. Quoting

81

God's own charges against him, Job owns up to his sin and resolves to move on:

> I know that thou canst do every thing, and that no thought can be withholden from thee. "Who is he that hideth counsel without knowledge?" therefore have I uttered that I understood not; things too wonderful for me, which I knew not. "Hear, I beseech thee, and I will speak: I will demand of thee, and declare thou unto me." I have heard of thee by the hearing of the ear: but now mine eye seeth thee. Wherefore I abhor myself, and repent in dust and ashes. (42:2–6)

The majesty, beauty, power, and intimate care of God revealed in the things He has made, and daily sustains, brings Job to his knees and turns him from sliding into sin to pursuing holiness before the Lord. It is reasonable to suppose that disciplining ourselves to discern the glory and grandeur of God in general revelation can have the same benefit for us, thus fulfilling one of God's purposes in so making Himself known.

Enhancing our witness. Finally, God intends His revelation of Himself in creation, culture, and the conscience to provide us with resources for our witness to Him:

> I will speak of the glorious honour of thy majesty, and of thy wondrous works. And men shall speak of the might of thy terrible acts: and I will declare thy greatness. They shall abundantly utter the memory of thy great goodness, and shall sing of thy righteousness. The LORD is gracious, and full of compassion; slow to anger, and of great mercy. The LORD is good to all: and his tender mercies are over all his works. All thy works shall praise thee, O LORD; and thy saints shall bless thee. (Ps. 145:5–10)

As we will see in part 3, Jonathan Edwards understood the power of general revelation to enhance the witness of Scripture concerning the living God. He, as well as anyone else in Christian history, embodies the realization of the psalmist's exhortation. We also may expect our witness to Christ to be enhanced as we bring into our presentation of the gospel light from general revelation to illustrate and bolster the testimony of God's Word and our own testimony. We are called to glorify

God in all things (1 Cor. 10:31). Effective use of God's general revelation can help us mightily in this high calling, as we will see in chapter 9.

General revelation is a potentially powerful resource for the life of faith. Neglecting the revelation of God in this area can lead to idolatry and sin. But taking up the study of general revelation, in the light of Scripture and according to the disciplines of creational theology, not only fulfills part of our reason for being, but enhances our knowledge of God, improves worship of Him, and aids us in our sanctification. We turn, then, to consider the disciplines of creational theology and how they may serve us in reading "the booke of the world."

Questions for Study or Discussion

1. In what ways would you like to see improvement in the expression, experience, and extension of worship in your life?

2. How might learning to perceive and experience God's revelation in creation, culture, and the actions of conscience help you to achieve these goals?

3. In which areas of your life do you sense a need to make progress in holiness? How are you currently pursuing this effort?

4. How might you expect the practice of creational theology to aid you in your sanctification?

5. Think of the people in your life who do not know the Lord. With which aspects of God's general revelation do they currently have daily contact? How might growing in your ability to see the Lord's glory in these areas help to make you more effective in bearing witness to them?

The Happy Task of Creational Theology

Activity 3

Continue making additional entries in your notebook. Pay attention to things that arrest your attention, or that provoke you to wonder, awe, or other strong sensations (sadness, joy, spontaneous delight, indignation, admiration, etc.). Note them as before. Choose one or two of these and set aside some time to meditate on the following:

- What about these perceptions or experiences can lead you to praise the Lord, or to intercede in prayer for others? Spend time doing so.
- Do these perceptions or experiences bring to mind any aspect(s) of your life that are standing in the way of your growing in grace? Can they serve to enhance your walk with the Lord in particular ways? Which?
- Meet with your conversation partner and share your conclusions from this activity.

4

CREATIONAL THEOLOGY

O LORD our Lord, how excellent is thy name in all the earth!
—Psalm 8:1

*And it is to be considered, that the more those divine
communications increase in the creature, the more it
becomes one with God: for so much the more is it
united to God in love, the heart is drawn nearer and
nearer to God, and the union with him becomes
more firm and close: and, at the same time, the creature becomes more and more conformed to God.*
—Jonathan Edwards[1]

As kingfishers catch fire, dragonflies draw flame;
As tumbled over rim in roundy wells
Stones ring; like each tucked string tells, each hung bell's
Bow swung finds tongue to fling out broad its name;
Each mortal thing does one thing and the same:
Deals out that being indoors each one dwells;
Selves—goes itself; *myself* it speaks and spells;
Crying *What I do is me: for that I came.*

85

I say more: the just man justices;
Keeps grace: that keeps all his goings graces;
Acts in God's eye what in God's eye he is—
Christ—for Christ plays in ten thousand places,
Lovely in limbs, and lovely in eyes not his
To the Father through the features of men's faces.

—*Gerard Manley Hopkins,* Sonnet 34

Before we look in more extensive detail at specific examples of Jonathan Edwards's use of the doctrine of general revelation, and at the creational-theology approach to that doctrine that characterizes his works, we would do well to consider the broad parameters and specific examples of the practice of creational theology.

Definition of Creational Theology

Creational theology is an attempt to improve our understanding and use of God's general revelation in creation, culture, and the actions of conscience. Creational theology involves the effort to bring the doctrine of general revelation into the household of faith in a more lively and beneficial manner, by improving our ability to understand and make better use of the book of the world according to the teaching of Scripture.

Consider Hopkins's poem quoted above. Throughout his ministry Hopkins was posted to the backwaters of British Roman Catholicism, among those his contemporaries would have regarded as the dregs of English and Irish society. His flocks were not what most would have considered the "beautiful people." They were, in many respects, unlovely and difficult to love. At first glance, like the dumb creatures of the impersonal world—kingfishers, dragonflies, stones, bells, and so on—they might have seemed insignificant beings, hardly worth noticing, who existed only to assert their individuality—which, in Victorian Britain, did not amount to much. But in the light of God's revelation in Scripture, Hopkins could see more. He observed the image of God in the mortals given into his charge, and saw in all their features the light of Jesus Christ Himself. He may have been thinking of a passage such as Matthew 25:40: " 'Verily I say unto you, Inasmuch as ye have done it unto one of the least of these my brethren, ye have done it unto me.' "

How often in the whirl and welter of pastoral duties are ministers of the gospel tempted to resent, neglect, or avoid the wearying, troublesome, or unsophisticated among their sheep? How common it is for Christians to treat one another in precisely the same manner. But Hopkins counsels us to observe people more deeply through the eyes of creational theology, seeing them as part of a grand divine creation where God is making Himself known, allowing the light of God's Word to illuminate our observations and to help us discern something more of God's revelation of Himself and His purposes and ways. Thus informed we may find love kindled within us, and our ministries refocused in the fuller and more complete light of the revelation of God in Scripture *and* creation. Such insight comes only from seeing ourselves, with others, as creatures of a loving Creator.

I do not claim that Hopkins or Cowper or, for that matter, Edwards was making conscious use of something called *creational theology*. I have coined this term in order to help the reader break free of the stereotypes associated with such terms as *general revelation, natural law*, and *natural theology*, and to avoid the culturally conditioned connotations of all uses of "nature" in referring to the *creation* of God. But I do insist that, consciously or not, these men, and others from the Christian tradition, understood and were making use of general revelation in ways different from, and vastly more beneficial than, the way many Christians typically do, to the extent that they do at all. By better understanding the use and the disciplines of creational theology as represented in the practice of these men, we might be able to improve our ability to decipher the glory and grandeur of God in general revelation in ways more in line with His purposes and goals in giving it.

In this chapter I want to summarize the presuppositions undergirding the practice of creational theology. Then we will examine the broad outlines and two illustrations of the practice of creational theology before proceeding, in part 3, to an examination of Edwards's use of this discipline. In part 4, our final section, we will look more closely at how to develop the specific disciplines outlined and illustrated both here and in the work of Edwards.

Presuppositions of Creational Theology

From what we have considered thus far, we can discern eight presuppositions for the work of creational theology as I am using the term here and as we will see it in the practice of Jonathan Edwards. These constitute the "base principles" that guide our use of the disciplines of this aspect of theological studies.

Christ Is the Way to the True Knowledge of God

In the first place, creational theology acknowledges that the revelation of God in Scripture informs us that the only way to the true knowledge of God is through the gospel of Jesus Christ. We cannot find our way to God through our own efforts, whether by reason, morality, or good intentions. The study of creation, culture, and the human conscience alone will not bring us to saving knowledge. Jesus Christ alone is the way to the Father (John 14:6); there is salvation in no other name but His (Acts 4:12). In the same way, unless we are continuing to grow in our relationship with Jesus Christ, we will not be able to make the best use of the theological discipline that we are calling creational theology.

This is the starting point for creational theology, and it makes this discipline the exclusive domain of those who have come to the saving knowledge of God in Jesus Christ and who inhabit the kingdom of light that is illuminated by His Word and Spirit (Col. 1:13–17; Eph. 5:8–10). Any attempts to make full and proper sense, from a theological or any other perspective, out of the data of creation will falter, and be less than God intends, unless they are grounded in and ordered according to the teaching of Scripture and the gospel of Jesus Christ.

This is not to say that unbelievers and others may not do valuable work in science, the arts, and so forth, or that they have not contributed some interesting and perhaps even useful insights about God from their work in these areas; it only insists that such work is incomplete at best. For the full and final purposes of creation to come to light, the things God has made must be considered through the eyes of faith in Jesus Christ.

At the same time, this presupposition reminds us that creational theology must not be taken up as a discipline unto itself. Creational theology is useful to the extent that it serves the purposes of the gospel in deepening our walk with the Lord, and in pointing others to Jesus Christ and leading them to a deeper knowledge of God through Him as well.

General Revelation Is True Revelation

Second, those who have been illuminated by Scripture and redeemed through Jesus Christ recognize that the revelation of God in Scripture further informs us that there is additional revelation from God in the creation around us—the creatures, cultures, and con-sciences of the peoples of the world. Through these means God is revealing His wisdom, goodness, and power for all to see. This is *real* revelation, as we have seen, not just subjective impressions. The glory of God revealed in these things can enhance our knowledge of God, draw us nearer to Him in worship, and shape and mold us into greater conformity to His image. The Spirit of God works through this gen-eral revelation and the glory revealed there, in the light of special rev-elation and the gospel, to mold us into greater degrees of Christlike-ness (2 Cor. 3:12–18).

The Lord Jesus and the apostles, as well as the writers of the Old Testament, were clear on this. This is why Scripture makes so many appeals to general revelation in preaching and teaching—in parables, illustrations, and images of a wide variety. The writers of Scripture, under the inspiration of the Holy Spirit, understood that appealing to such things could be greatly used of God in helping redeemed people come to true understanding about Him, His purposes, and His ways. That is no less true for us today than it was in the days when God was inspiring writers to give His revelation in His Word.

General Revelation Can Be Appreciated Only by the Redeemed

In the third place, those who have come into the light of the gospel understand from God's Word that, although this powerful revelation from creation comes clearly and compellingly to all people, only those who have been renewed in Christ will be able to recognize it for what it is and make use of it as God intends. All others, being in a rebellious and unregenerate state, though they see this revelation and may attain to a certain real and true knowledge of God through it, nonetheless suppress that knowledge in unrighteous deeds and turn to a life of ingratitude, idolatry, disobedience, and self-destruction (Rom. 1:18–32). This follows from what we have said above about the knowledge of God—which is the purpose of theological studies—being available only through faith in Jesus Christ. Lost people will not come to the knowledge of God that He is revealing in the creation, so that they might seek further and even saving knowledge of Him, as He intends (Acts 17:24–27). Therefore, they cannot be expected to plumb the depths of meaning in general revelation, except as the grace of God works with the gospel to bring them to saving truth.

At one level, therefore, it might appear that any and all appeals to the revelation of God in creation will be futile, perhaps even harmful to the unregenerate, leading to further hardening of the heart. But as we will see, this is not entirely true; God is at work calling His elect to salvation, and it pleases Him for us to use general revelation in that great work, as Edwards will show us.

The Redeemed Must Make Proper Use of General Revelation

Fourth, the redeemed of the Lord may not ignore the fact of God's revelation in the creation, and so must search out its proper use. Scripture shows them that the proper use of God's revelation in creation depends on, in the first instance, acknowledging God as Creator and ourselves and all other things as His creatures. He has made us, and not we ourselves (Ps. 100:3). His purposes inform and guide all that is and everything that transpires (Ps. 29; Eph. 1:11). In all that exists, therefore, there is something to be discerned concerning God's deity, purposes, truth, or ways. In discerning this revelation of God, the redeemed hope to increase in knowledge of and love for Him, and to bring their own lives into greater conformity with His will, in agreement with God's purposes for so revealing Himself, as we have seen.

The Redeemed Accept the Challenge of General Revelation

Fifth, for the sake of growing in grace and improving knowledge of God, the redeemed accept the responsibility and happy task of pursuing the knowledge of God that the creation is declaring (Ps. 111:2; Eccl. 1:13). As with the study of Scripture, the redeemed of the Lord will give themselves to careful study, by perceiving and experiencing the works of God in creation, culture, and the ways of conscience, expecting thereby to grow in knowledge of and love for God, and in conformity to His image. And they will undertake these studies as theological disciplines, that is, as efforts to improve knowledge of God, to grow in love for Him and others, and to become increasingly conformed to His image.

Scripture Is the Only Final, Reliable Guide to Creational Theology

Sixth, the redeemed recognize that this task can be accomplished only in the light of Scripture and under the guidance of the Spirit of God. Guided by Scripture and the Holy Spirit, the redeemed work to discover the light of truth in creation and, by so doing, to love God more (Ps. 36:9; John 16:13). This work, they understand, is best accomplished as a community endeavor, in which God's people work together on the foundation of His Word—especially according to the disciplines of biblical and systematic theology—to teach and admonish one another from the fuller revelation of God in Scripture and creation (1 Cor. 12:7–11; Eph. 2:18–22; Col. 3:16; Heb. 10:24). The redeemed must pool their resources, share their perspectives, and be willing both to teach and to learn if the work of creational theology is to realize its promise (Col. 3:16).

General Revelation Can Aid in Proclamation

Seventh (and as we will see further later on), the redeemed recognize that among the unregenerate are a vast number of God's elect—

as many as the stars of heaven and the sands of the seas—and that God's Spirit is striving with and wooing these whom God has loved from before the foundation of the world. They therefore follow the example of Scripture and, in the light of Scripture and the gospel, appeal to the revelation of God in creation to aid in igniting the spark of true religion in the unregenerate elect. God has chosen these lost ones and is working to draw them to Himself, effectually calling them to salvation through the light of the gospel of Jesus Christ and the work of His Spirit. The effect of a right use of creational theology with the unregenerate elect can help summon the knowledge of God in their hearts, heighten their sense of His existence and majesty, warn them of His wrath, and further prepare their hearts for the work of the Spirit in the proclamation of the gospel.[2] The biblical doctrine of election allows us to qualify the conclusion to the third point above so that we may make good and wise use of the revelation of God in creation in our work of preaching and evangelism.

At the same time, and as a kind of corollary to this presupposition, creational theology can kindle the flame of love for God more fervently in the hearts of the redeemed, an assumption that follows both from this presupposition and from the second point.

Creational Theology Can Harden as Well as Woo

Finally, the redeemed acknowledge as well that appealing to the revelation of God in creation among the unregenerate can also lead to the further hardening of those marked out for eternal condemnation (Acts 17:32–34). Our inability to persuade all the lost through the use of general revelation with the gospel—indeed, the tendency of such appeals to harden certain people all the more—is thus no failure of mission or technique on our part. Instead, it is a confirmation of the teaching of Scripture and further proof of the reliability of God's Word as He hardens those He will harden against the saving knowledge of Christ (Rom. 9:18).

Thus, as the redeemed grow in their understanding of the revelation of God in creation, and as they encourage one another in love and good works on the basis of all that God is revealing about Himself,

His purposes, His truth, and His ways, they do not hesitate to bring the full weight of God's revelation, whether in Scripture or creation, to bear on the task of proclaiming the truth of Jesus Christ. They do not rely on general revelation alone as a kind of bridge to a general knowledge of God, and from there to the gospel, but only appeal to it with the gospel, and in the light of the gospel, for they recognize that only the gospel can lead to the saving knowledge of God. And yet, no matter how skillful their use of this discipline, many of those they seek to reach will grow even more hardened against the gospel. In this, however, we do not despair, or seek more "evidence" to try to convince others. Instead, we glory in such manifestations of the truth of God, continue loving even our enemies, and go on seeking God's elect through the proclamation of His truth.

We are well advised to keep these presuppositions in mind as we take up the task of creational theology. They can help to keep us from drifting into the mistakes of both the maximizers and minimizers of general revelation, and guide us in making proper use of the revelation of God's glory in the things He has made.

The Practice of Creational Theology: Two Certainties

I frequently ponder what it might have been like to be standing alongside God for the duration of the creation week, especially as He was rendering those numerous intermittent assessments of His work, pronouncing it "good." In considering this setting, we encounter some very important principles about the created world, its nature and purpose, and the promise it holds for revealing God to us.

Is it not curious that God pauses to evaluate His work of creation as it proceeds through the six days of Genesis 1? Like an artist stepping back from the easel, head cocked and one eye closed, thumb halfway up the brush and lined up like the sight of a gun, God declares His work-in-progress to be pleasing to Him. It is what He wants it to be; it "speaks" what He wants it to speak. The line going out from His creation says that it is good—and, at the last, very good (Gen. 1:31), a perfect reflection of His intentions and desires.

93

What God saw in His creation was a reflection of Himself. He observed something in the work of His hands that pleased Him because it manifested Him, or at least it expressed what He desired for His creation to His complete satisfaction. David Atkinson writes concerning these pronouncements of God:

> This is the basis for a celebration and enjoyment of God's world, which in some Christian teaching has got lost behind an almost exclusive emphasis on sin. Art and music, drama and dance can all be used to celebrate the goodness of God's world . . . We need to recover a sense of delight in good things, even though, as we shall see from Genesis 3, there is also a shadow.[3]

What did God—and what might we—observe in His work of creation? Images of harmony amid diversity; order superintending a plurality of forms; hierarchies of value; hints of as-yet-undisclosed beauty and goodness; contrasts and combinations of light and color; progress and development; simplicity in the midst of complexity; man and woman as the crown of creation; community and mutual concern; love and covenant obedience; and in and through it all the attending grace of God by His Spirit and Word. All these images suggest insights concerning God, His purpose, His truth, and His ways that can guide us in further understanding His revelation in Scripture, as well as in enhancing our walk with Him and our witness to the lost. The "good" creation in all its aspects can speak to us of the beauty, goodness, and truth of God. But if it is to do so, we must keep in mind two certainties and be willing to adhere to two guiding principles.

The Manifest Goodness of God

The first certainty is that God's line is going forth in all the works of His hand, and we believe that He is speaking through the creation some very powerful truths about Himself. It is the happy task of creational theology to teach us, through perceiving and experiencing creation, to observe those truths and benefit from them. Cowper writes of the Christian:

He looks abroad into the varied field
Of nature, and though poor, perhaps, compared
With those whose mansions glitter in his sight,
Calls the delightful scenery all his own.
His are the mountains, and the valleys his,
And the resplendent rivers. His to enjoy
With a propriety that none can feel
But who, with filial confidence inspired,
Can lift to heaven an unpresumptuous eye,
And smiling say—"My Father made them all!"

—*The Task, 5.738–47*

Had we been alongside our Father during that creation week, like Cowper's observer of the "varied field / Of nature," we would have agreed completely with His assessment, as we perceived and experienced the beauty, symmetry, diversity, potency, and overall harmony and majesty of the creation. We would have recognized these attributes as characterizing the Creator as well, and revealing something of His will for us.

The Tragedy of the Fall

Why is it, then, that people have such a hard time seeing God, being convinced of His existence, and learning about Him from the works of His hands? As David Atkinson indicated, it is because of the second certainty, the tragedy of the fall. As we have seen, when people "hear" God speaking His line to them through the things He has made, they turn a deaf ear to Him, suppressing whatever knowledge of Him they may possess and turning away from Him to the worship of false idols—created things of all sorts, including work, wealth, leisure, fame, and sex (Rom. 1:18–21).

But what of those who have come to know the Lord through the redemption He has provided in Jesus Christ? Do they sense that "filial confidence" that allows them to see their Lord in the works of His hands? Do they not have the potential for observing in the things of God's creation the goodness that gave Him such delight? Most emphatically, yes, in spite of the continuing effects of the fall. Indeed, the creation itself longs to be thus properly perceived and experienced (Rom. 8:19–21).

Yet there seems to be so little celebrating of the beauty and wonder of God in the creation among contemporary Christians—not much poetry, little in the way of artistic expression, few conversations or discussions, and only a trickle of music, drama, or dance celebrating the glory of God revealed in the creation around us. Certainly not much reflection on the glories of the creation finds its way into the formal theological works and seminary training on which we rely in preparing the leaders of our churches. As Dallas Willard has observed, "We are showered with messages that simply go right through or past us. We are not *attuned* to God's voice."[4] Perhaps this explains why there is little celebration of God's revelation of Himself through the creation in the piety and devotions of individual believers. Here is God, working continuously, sending out His line throughout the creation to reveal His goodness to us, and we seem unable or unwilling to study His works in order to see what He might be saying to us. Why is this?

I suspect it is because our approach to knowing God—our approach, that is, to doing theology—has been so limited to the logical and verbal that we have not felt the need for learning how to perceive and experience His revelation of Himself in the creation around us. But God calls us to study His works, as we have seen. We have fallen short of God's plan for our theological work, and in so falling short of His glory, we show the lingering effects of sin in our lives (Rom. 3:23). Our ability to do theology through perception and experience—to do creational theology—is weak and undeveloped compared to our ability to deduce theological conclusions from the study of Scripture and through discussion, dialogue, and debate. It is instructive to be reminded, from Psalm 106, that Israel fell into rebellion and disobedience whenever it failed to contemplate the works of God that He had undertaken on their behalf to make Himself known. If our work in theology and consequently our knowledge of and love for the Lord are to be more complete, then we must learn to "hear" what He would say to us through the things He has made as well, always reflecting on our perceptions and experiences in that realm in the light of the more perfect revelation of Himself that God has provided for us in His Word. This work begins with learning how to perceive and experience the created order so as to discern the line of God going out through it. The heavens are telling the glories of God, displaying His goodness, majesty, power, and love, and revealing things about His ways and His desires for His creatures. As Alexander Schmemann has observed: "All that exists is God's gift to man, and it all exists to make God known, to make man's life communion with God . . . God *blesses* everything He creates, and, in biblical language, this means that He makes all creation the sign and means of His presence and wisdom, love and revelation."[5]

Therefore, let us repent of our neglect of this potentially powerful discipline of creational theology and resolve that we will take up this calling with as much fervor as we do that of seeking the glory of God in His Word. As we engage in the happy task of creational theology and begin to perceive and experience God's revelation of Himself in the creation around us, we will find that our understanding of Him and His ways will be greatly enhanced and that our love for Him will grow more and more. These are His goals for thus revealing Himself, and we have every reason to expect that if we are diligent in our calling, He will fulfill the promise of His revelation.

The Practice of Creational Theology: Two Principles

Job's defense against the false charges of his erstwhile friends included the plea that he had "made a covenant" with his eyes so that he would not look upon a young woman to lust after her (Job 31:1). We may discern in this covenant two principles for learning to perceive and experience the creation around us through the disciplines of creational theology.

A Conscious Decision

First, Job made a conscious decision to use his eyes in a way that would be pleasing to the Lord. He understood that lusting for another woman was wrong, that employing his eyes for such a purpose was not pleasing to God and would not be of benefit to himself or his marriage. So he decided that he would not allow his eyes to be used in a lustful way.

Besides being an excellent guideline for dealing with temptation, Job's decision concerning his eyes is instructive for us in learning to perceive and experience the revelation of God in the creation around us. We must make up our minds that we are going to seek the Lord with our eyes, as well as all our other senses. We must make a commitment to engage our senses in trying to discern His revelation in the things of the creation around us. We must "covenant with our eyes" to look for the line that the Lord is sending out concerning His goodness in all the things of the creation that we will encounter throughout the day.

This commitment must not be merely for a certain period. Would we make such a commitment concerning the Word of God? "For the next year I resolve before You, O Lord, to study Your Word as often as I can, so that I might get to know You better." Then, after a year, we could get back to whatever else we were doing. Hardly. God calls us to seek out His glory wherever He is revealing it, to seek Him with all our hearts and to keep on seeking until He makes Himself ever more clearly known (Ps. 63:1–2; Jer. 29:13; Matt. 7:7–11, esp. v. 11). The commitment we make to seeking the Lord in the things He has made will require us to reevaluate our priorities and revise our practices, as we will see in part 4.

An Embrace of Disciplines

Second, Job's covenant with his eyes, in and of itself, would not have made much of a difference in the way he looked upon a young woman unless he also cultivated the disciplines necessary for carrying out his covenant daily. Doubtless Job came into contact with many young women. He would have appreciated much about their beauty, wit, and charm. But he would not allow his mind to wander into the darker regions of lust and vain imaginations, for he had made a covenant with his eyes not to do that. We can only imagine how he handled this, what disciplines he fell back on to accomplish his resolution. Perhaps, while talking with a young woman, he trained himself not to be distracted by her outward beauty and charm, knowing these to be deceptive, fading, and fleeting, inner beauty being the only true and lasting thing. Perhaps he was even more guarded, not allowing himself to be alone with a woman other than his wife for any reason. We don't know; we can only speculate. But in some way, when push came to shove, Job, remembering his covenant with his eyes, then disciplined his eyes to perceive and his mind to experience in such a way as to enable him to remain blameless before the Lord.

We, too, must learn some new disciplines if we are going to be able to carry out our resolution to seek the Lord in the things He has made. My purpose in this chapter is primarily to illustrate those disciplines at work. In part 3 we will look to the example of Jonathan Edwards, to discover in more detail the uses of creational theology and the benefits that can come from practicing these disciplines with greater faithfulness. Then, in part 4, we will unpack the disciplines of creational theology in more detail. For now, we're interested merely in reaching some resolution to take up this work, together with a willingness to embrace the disciplines it will entail, so that God's general revelation can lead us into the fuller, richer perception and experience of His glory and grandeur.

But *where* do we look?

The Practice of Creational Theology: Three Foci

We have repeatedly said that God is revealing His glory in all the works of His hands. This includes His work of creation, or what is normally referred to as "nature"; the culture by which people define, enrich, and sustain themselves; and the actions that proceed from the workings of their consciences.

Look to Creation, Not "Nature"

We have already argued the first point perhaps sufficiently well: God is revealed in the trees, mountains, seasons, wildlife, processes, and "laws" of the created order. Very few will have any difficulty with this idea.

99

What may be difficult for many of us is breaking out of the inherited cultural practice of referring to such things as "nature." Alister McGrath has shown how culturally loaded and "socially mediated," and thus unstable and unclear, this concept can be.[6] "Nature" implies neutral, ungrounded reality—stuff of various kinds—existing, as it were, by itself, waiting to be discovered, defined, and deployed according to whatever social purposes or worldview may have possession of it at any given time. Such a view is rendered invalid by the presuppositions outlined above. What is commonly called "nature" "is a socially mediated concept . . . necessarily viewed through a prism of beliefs and values."[7] The beliefs and values outlined above, through which we approach such things, seem to preclude "going along" with common practice and referring to matter that has been created by God, is sustained by God, and reflects His glory by so culturally loaded a term as "nature." As the authors of *Redeeming Creation* boldly insist, "one of the central teachings of [Scripture] is that the natural world is not at all natural. It is the creation of a supernatural God. What we routinely call 'nature' is in fact 'creation.' "[8] McGrath writes, "The Christian approach to nature is to see it as God's creation."[9] We must develop the practice of referring to those phenomena that we profess to have been created by God and that we recognize as being sustained by Him—and are thus vessels of His revelation—as "creation," and to the raft of disciplines that help to get at this revelation as "creational theology."

Look to Culture

Second, we expect to see the glory of God in aspects of human culture. What I would describe as my first encounter with the living God came in the presence of a marvelous artifact of human culture. It was prom night, 1967, and my friend Jim Hentzel and I and our dates were having dinner at a boring French restaurant across the interstate from Lambert St. Louis Airport. We pondered what we might do to "liven up" the evening and make it a little more memorable. Almost simultaneously the thought came to Jim and me, and we exclaimed as one, "Gateway Arch!" The Arch at that time was nearing completion. The exterior was finished, but the innards still had to be built and the landscaping put in. The Arch was surrounded by a plastic construction fence and gobs of signs warning, "Stay Out." No matter. Over the fence, across the field of dirt clods, and up to the very base of the Arch we ran. I stood at the southern leg and stretched my hands out to embrace the stainless-steel structure, looking up its 630-foot height as I did so. Suddenly I was overwhelmed by a sense of transcendence. The beauty of the structure, its smooth, cool texture, and the wonder of artistic vision and engineering expertise that had produced it all rushed into my brain at once. I felt that I was in the presence of something larger than life, something wondrous, beautiful, and enduring—I felt that I was in the presence of God. Though not a believer at that time, I was profoundly affected by the experience. I have never forgotten it.

Culture consists of the artifacts, institutions, and conventions by which people define, sustain, and enrich themselves. Culture includes the arts, law, languages, economies, philosophies of teaching and learning, family life, community traditions, and much more. All culture ultimately derives from the fact that people are created in the image of God and gifted by Him in many and varied ways. After all, the psalmist tells us, God has given gifts of all kinds to all kinds of people, even those who are in rebellion against Him, with the idea that He might express Himself through those gifts, as they are brought to bear on the task of creating culture. Since I have argued this point in sufficient detail elsewhere, I will not repeat that discussion here.[10] I just want to reiterate that as we study aspects of human culture, we expect to see glimmers, be they ever so faint, of divine glory, revealing to us something about God and His truth, purposes, and ways.

Look to the Conscience

Finally, those actions of people that arise from the condition of their consciences can also be a source of general revelation. In his book *What We Can't Not Know*,[11] J. Budziszewski shows the powerful effects of the knowledge of the works of the law of God on the consciences of men and women. People make their foundational choices in life on the basis of how they respond to that law, whether in agreement and obedience or in denial and rebellion. Ultimately, all human action derives from the conscience, which works in the soul to process the knowledge of the mind and the affections of the heart into actions by word and deed. As Jesus said, the words and deeds of men derive from the goings-on in their souls, where the conscience brings heart and mind together either in agreement with the works of God's law written on it or in rebellion against that law (Rom. 2:14–15). As we observe those actions of the conscience, we should expect to see some aspect of God's being, purposes, or truth reflected in them.

A couple of examples: Jesus saw in the conduct of the religious leaders of His day that their consciences were obedient to Satan, rather than God. He told them that they were sons of their father, the devil. But this did not alarm Him; rather, it simply confirmed what He understood of the teaching of Scripture and guided Him in His demeanor vis-à-vis the scribes and Pharisees. Peter, writing to churches that had begun to come under persecution, discerned in the actions of their tormentors the good hand of God moving to strengthen them in their faith (1 Peter 1:6–7). The writer of Hebrews saw in the troubles that his readers were experiencing at the hands of unbelievers the chastening of God warning them not to fall away from true faith in Christ (Heb. 12:4–15). So also we, by observing the actions of conscience in the light of Scripture, may hope to discover something of God or His purposes, truth, or ways there.

In creation, culture, and the actions of conscience, we may expect to be confronted by the glory of God as He reveals something to us about Himself and His ways. If we are going to begin discerning the Lord's line in the created world around us, we will need not only to make up our minds to do so, but to discipline our eyes to look for the revelation of God in creation, culture, and the actions of conscience. In the remainder of this chapter, I want to provide two illustrations of the shape that such investigations might take and of how we might expect to benefit from learning to practice creational theology.

102

The Practice of Creational Theology: Two Examples

Under the Trees of Mamre

A fascination with trees. Just south of the Pennsylvania state line on U.S. Highway 1 is the Spready Oak Diner, where, if you order your hamburger any way other than well done, you have to sign for it. The huge, sprawling oak from which the diner takes its name—and that is memorialized on the sign out front—is long since dead, but the enormous stump is preserved in the yard, just beyond the parking lot.

On the noise barriers that line Route 202 along Philadelphia's western suburbs—those ugly aggregate walls that give homeowners a sense of distance from the traffic rumbling just beyond their backyards—trees stand out in bas-relief, sculpted, no doubt, at some considerable expense. Are they there to make the walls themselves look more like natural parts of the environment, or to soothe drivers growing increasingly irritated by the lumbering traffic?

When my family moved from Florida to Pennsylvania to take up a ministry in the suburbs of Philadelphia, one of the houses we looked at had an enormous oak tree in the front yard. It was reputed to be the oldest tree in the county, and I confess to having given that house—otherwise rather plain and too expensive—special consideration because of that fact alone. We ended up buying a house nestled into a grove of oak trees, which we named, appropriately, Oak Grove.

People have always been fascinated with trees and have depended on them in many ways. We look upon them with awe and reverence for their majesty and mystery, and we treasure them for their economic potential. We decorate our homes and properties with flowering trees of all sorts. Farmers and landscapers depend on them to keep soil in place against the ravages of wind and rain. Eco-warriors risk fines and imprisonment to save them from greedy capitalists. The economy of my former state of West Virginia is highly dependent on the timber harvested from trees. Some tree gave its all so that you could read the printed pages of this book.

Trees in tradition and Scripture. Primitive peoples regarded trees as meeting places between heaven and earth, and used them as rallying points for religious gatherings or considered them the homes of local deities. Sacred trees and groves abound in the folk literature of peoples throughout the world, as well as in the pages of Scripture. The monasteries of sixth-century Celtic saints Brigit, at Kildare (Church of the Oaks), and Columba, at Derry (The Oaks), both former pagan centers of worship, illustrate the Celtic Christian penchant for taking pagan practices captive and making them serve the purposes of Christ. We have seen how Job saw in the life cycle of trees a source of hope, a parable suggestive of the reality of new life beyond death (Job 14:7–10).

It was probably the most natural thing in the world for Abram, the son of idol-worshipers, to establish his base in a new land amid the groves of Mamre, and to wait there for God to give him further instructions (Gen. 12:6; 18:1; 23:17). Perhaps this place was recognized by local peoples as having religious significance, a place where one might go to meet with God. Maybe it was recommended to Abram by one of the locals when he or she came to understand the nature of this stranger's business among them. We can imagine Abram standing beneath some great oak, swooning in the awe of its majesty and the refreshing coolness of its shade, and looking up along its mighty trunk toward heaven, wondering whether God would reveal to him any more of His covenant plan. In His mercy God condescended to Abram's lingering pagan consciousness and spoke to him there, under the trees of Mamre, whereupon Abram built an altar to the Lord on that spot and worshiped Him.

The Scriptures frequently encourage us to regard trees as indicators of the favor and glory of God. It was trees, after all, including those beautiful to look upon, that God first appointed for the sustenance, aesthetic training, and testing-ground of Adam and Eve (Gen. 2:8–17). God promised abundant fruit from all sorts of trees as a result of Israel's obedience to His covenant (Lev. 26:4); yet those same trees would be sterile and fruitless during periods of Israel's disobedience, indicating God's displeasure (Lev. 26:20). The trees, we are told, will sing praises to God in the time of His revealing Himself (1 Chron. 16:33). The fruit trees are called upon along with the cedars to join in praising God as part of creation's chorus of glory (Ps. 148:9). The trees of the field will clap their hands with joy when the people of God come to know His saving grace (Isa. 55:12). It was a fig tree that Jesus withered for its failure to provide food when He came seeking it (Matt. 21:18–20), thus employing it as a symbol of the barrenness of Israel. And it is for the tree of life on either side of the river of the water of life that we are encouraged to hope as the landmark of our final dwelling place with God (Rev. 22:2).

God's line going out in the trees. Clearly God's line is going out among the trees of the field. We should expect, therefore, that careful observation of a tree or a stand of trees might have something to reveal to us about the God who made trees and who continues to sustain them by the Word of His power (Heb. 1:3). As part of His good creation, trees bear the stamp of God's handiwork (Gen. 1:31). Thus, they can help to enrich our understanding of their Creator and His ways, and can encourage us to esteem Him more highly and to love Him more fully. We only have to discipline our eyes to observe them as aspects of God's general revelation.

Yet so commonplace are trees that at first we may have difficulty in "hearing" the message they have for us concerning their Creator and ours. And the idea of "hugging a tree" strikes most of us as just a bit strange.

Well, I'm not recommending that you hug a tree, although I would not be surprised if, after taking time to contemplate the line of God going out through the trees, you might feel like doing so. For the trees of the field can "speak" to us about the goodness of God. They can help us to understand His ways and His plan for creation. By carefully observing trees in their environment, we can come "to comprehend and better appreciate just how nature works"[12] and, in so doing, how God has designed all His creation to function to His praise and glory. All that is required is that we be willing to take the time to look, and that we analyze our observations in the light of what God has revealed about Himself in His Word (Ps. 36:9).

The visible aspects of a tree. As you approach a tree to begin observing it, three aspects immediately present themselves. First is the tree's size. Especially if you have chosen a large tree—an oak, poplar, or large pine, for example—let yourself be impressed with this living thing standing ten or twenty times your own height. Then recall that the trees, like everything else in the creation, were put here by God for our enjoyment and use (Gen. 1:26–28; 2:8–9). Trees, besides being beautiful to look at, produce as much as 20 percent of the oxygen on earth, thus helping to keep the air sufficiently clean and rich to sustain all other life.[13] A large tree is a handsome and sophisticated oxygen-producing factory, living and working in an unending shift in order to make it possible for people and other creatures to live and work as well. Here it stands, waving gently in the breeze, towering high above you, impressive, perhaps even awesome, in its height, yet it is your servant, put there by God to make your life better and more enjoyable (Ps. 119:90–91). In this regard, trees remind me of the angels: awesome, impressive, spiritual creatures, who nonetheless exist to serve the needs of God's people, and serve God Himself, who is continuously at work guarding the welfare of His people (Ps. 121:3–4).

Second, you will be impressed by its symmetry. Most trees, if they have not been damaged by storm, disease, or telephone linemen, reveal a symmetry, a balance that spreads out along the central trunk fairly equally in all directions. The trunk is round, as is the tree itself, which you could easily guess, and which you could see by imagining that you are looking at it from above or as a landscaper might draw it on a diagram for positioning in your yard. The tree is easy to look at and provides a pleasing object of concentration for the eyes, not ragged, jagged, and uneven, as if defying us to find some inherent patterns or overall definition. The tree is a study of beauty in simplicity, suggesting the larger beauty and balance of the ecosystem in which it exists, and that is sustained by God. He makes things beautiful. He keeps them beautiful. He employs them for our well-being and for the revelation of His glory, who is Himself all beauty and goodness.

Third, there is the complexity in what you see. A tree is made up of a trunk, numerous branches of various sizes, and either leaves or needles of uniform size and shape. It displays a variety of colors—

shades of green, gray, and brown, too many to try to catalogue. Each part of the tree has its own unique and important function in the life of the tree and the environment around it. And a tree is not a static creature: its leaves shimmer, its branches bend and bow, and its trunk sways gently in the breeze. It is alive, simple yet complex, beautiful yet hard at work to serve the larger purposes of God in bringing goodness and blessing to His creation.

Already in what you see of the tree your theological mind should be engaged with thoughts of the grandeur, goodness, mercy, wisdom, and lovingkindness of the Lord, and of the power of sin in human life. He is a God of order, who rules His creation not capriciously, but in a way that makes it possible for us to understand and rule over it, and thus to benefit from it even as we care for the creation in a manner that imitates God's own. That at times people have been so cavalier in their regard for trees, so selfish in wantonly destroying them for material gain, testifies to the sinfulness with which we have regarded so much of God's creation in our state of rebellion against Him. God has given us trees to use, it is true, but the widespread destruction of the forests of the earth should cause us to reflect on the power of greed in human endeavor.

The tree puts us in mind of the nature of God Himself. He is one God but diverse in Persons, each of the members of the Trinity having His own role in the work of God, just like the trunk, branches, and leaves of a tree. Just as each of those parts contains all the "treeness" of the tree itself, each of the Persons of the Godhead shares in all the essential attributes of God, at the same time retaining His own unique Personhood and calling. The ubiquity of trees, which all too often leads us to take them for granted, reminds us that God is ever present with us, always providing for our needs and taking care of us in unseen—and too frequently unacknowledged—ways. The way in which trees strain toward the light, reaching upward toward the heavens, exposing as many as possible of their leaves to the sun and growing straight toward it, reminds us that we were made for the Light of God and should ever strive to grow toward it more and more ourselves. The blessing that trees provide to their environment should cause us to remember that God has called us to be blessings as well. To stand directly under a large tree, both hands on its trunk, and then to lean back and look upward along the trunk is to experience something of the strength and majesty of God. At the same time, it can remind us of Christ's death on the cursed tree for our transgressions.

The unseen aspects of a tree. All these things that we can see of a tree provide many opportunities for growing in and celebrating the knowledge of God. But a tree is more than simply what we see by direct observation. Many of a tree's components and activities can enrich our knowledge of God and His ways with people, but can become "visible" only through more careful observation, for example, through reading and study.

Consider, in the first place, the root system of the tree. Nearly as high and as far spread as the tree stands above ground, its roots extend below the earth, holding the tree in place, firming up the ground for us to stand and build on, enriching the soil with the by-products of its own internal processes, and deriving from the soil what it needs to sustain its own growth. The unseen roots remind us that much that is essential for our well-being goes on around us in the unseen world of spiritual realities. We cannot see the roots of the tree, but the tree could not exist without them. Indeed, nor could we. In the same way, we cannot see the angels protecting and defending us, nor the Spirit of God constantly attending to us (Pss. 91:11; 139:7–12), but without them we would be undone in a moment (Job 34:14–15). The spiritual realm is inaccessible to our eyes, but it is nonetheless real, and we could not get through a single day without the help, strength, and support we derive from these unseen realities. The unseen roots of a tree can help to keep us mindful of such eternal verities.

Beneath the surface of the tree—in its trunk, branches, and leaves—a dizzyingly complex variety of activities goes on continuously. Roger Caras describes these for us:

The tree was a perfect combination of elements, each of them reflecting the years of the giant's growing. In the center lay the heartwood. It was the supporting column of the mature tree. Heartwood is dead, it cannot grow, but it will not decay or fail the tree by losing strength as

108

long as the rest of the tree remains intact and in balance with its sur-
roundings. Girding the central column was the sapwood. Through it
ran the pipelines that carried water from the roots to the leaves. As the
inner layers of sapwood lose their vitality, they join the center column
as heartwood. Surrounding the sapwood was a thin but vital layer
known as the cambium. Each year, stimulated by auxins, or hormones,
this layer produces both new bark and new sapwood on its outer and
inner surfaces. Lying outside the cambium layer was the part of the tree
known as the phloem. Just as the sapwood carried water from the roots
to the leaves, the phloem carried food down from the leaves to the rest
of the tree. As growth continued within the cambium layer, the phloem
was pushed out to become true bark. And beyond the phloem was that
bark, the means by which the tree protected itself against heat and cold
and some enemies.[14]

Meanwhile, in the leaves, a pigment called chlorophyll is absorb-
ing light and mixing it with water and carbon dioxide from the air to
produce the material of life that the tree requires in order to grow. The
by-product of this process of photosynthesis is the oxygen we breathe,
which is exhausted by the leaves into the surrounding air. Leaves capture, store, and pass along the energy of the sun, making maximum
use of all available light for the production of food and oxygen in an
unseen process that is essential to the sustenance of life on our planet.
At even smaller levels—microscopic levels—still more remarkable
processes are at work, as the cells of a tree divide, multiply, and grow.
But the variety of activities taking place, the diversity of "instruments"
involved—large and small, strong and frail—and the results that they
together produce suggest some things to the theologically minded about
the God they serve and the ways He relates to them.

Such considerations should lead our thoughts especially to the body
of Christ, which comprises many members, some great, some small,
but each with different callings, and all essential to the well-being of
the whole and the fulfillment of the church's mission on earth. The
church is like a tree, made up of many differently gifted members linked
together in an organic whole that is intended by God to nurture and
strengthen itself at the same time that it brings blessing to the community of which it is a part. Some members have large, visible tasks;

109

yet they could not accomplish these unless smaller, less visible members were supporting them in their own individual works of service. No tree trunk can stand, mighty, impressive, and strong, without the cambium and sapwood and the innumerable cells of which they are composed. Similarly, no eloquent preacher, powerful evangelist, or effective missionary can do his or her work without the support in prayer, giving, and unseen collaboration of many other members of the body of Christ. That body will grow stronger as each member discerns his or her own unique gifts and finds a place to serve for the common good (1 Cor. 12:4–26). The church today stands by the support of generations long since dead, who, like the dead heartwood of a tree, provide the strength and direction upon which we build in our own generation, and whose vitality survives as long as we continue to protect and preserve the memory of those who have gone before us in the faith. Thus, continuously strengthened as each part does its work, the church is able to shade the surrounding community with the grace and goodness of God, bear fruit for its nourishment, and enrich the social, cultural, and moral air with the sweet fragrance of the love of Christ.

Stand beneath a tree, like Abram amid the trees in the plain of Mamre. Wait upon the Lord there, and discipline your eyes to observe carefully. Let the tree "speak" to you its own line in the revelation of God's goodness and glory. Then, don't just hug the tree; rather, like Abram, filled with the wonder of divine self-disclosure, worship God with an offering of thanksgiving and praise—God who makes Himself known to us and tells us of His glory in the trees of the field. And let each subsequent tree you encounter throughout the day be an ambassador of glory and a summons to praise and thanksgiving for the God who gives such servants to His people. We should not need, like Job in his confrontation with the living God, some oral revelation from heaven to prompt us to look for the knowledge of God in the things He has made. His line is constantly going out in them. By covenanting with our eyes to be careful observers of the natural world, we may expect to grow in our ability to discern what God is saying to us through the things He has made.

110

God and God's Truth in the Bookstore

"A good bookstore is one of the most comforting places on earth."[15] Also one in which we may expect to grow in theological understanding and the knowledge of God. Bookstores are becoming increasingly prominent features on the cultural landscape of America's cities. I have loved bookstores since childhood, when, as often as my father would take me downtown, I would wander into Graham's Book Store to look at the books and magazines offered there. My interest at that time was primarily sports, so I would thumb through the latest issues of every sports magazine on the rack, or look through a book on some sport or other. I remember, on one occasion, purchasing a small book about Boston Celtic guard Bob Cousy, which I read over and over as a child. On another visit I bought a book about Yankee slugger Roger Maris, the contents of which I can recall nothing today. If you had asked me in those days what the function of bookstores was, I would have told you that they existed to feed my hunger for and to help me develop my understanding and skills in the various sports in which I was involved. If you had observed me on those occasions when I was present in Graham's Book Store, you would have reached a similar conclusion.

More than books to observe. Today, however, whenever I enter a bookstore, my eyes are trained for different purposes. Certainly I love to look at books—to handle them, thumb through the pages, read the contents and skim the indexes, and so forth. But I almost never buy books at a bookstore, odd as that may seem, since they can be secured more cheaply through book clubs or the Internet. Yet I still frequent bookstores as often as I can, not just to look at books or for the pleasant ambience of words and knowledge, but to see what I might discern about the interests of my contemporaries and what that might tell me about the ways of God with men. William Cowper was right when he observed concerning books:

> Books are not seldom talismans and spells
> By which the magic art of shrewder wits
> Holds an unthinking multitude enthrall'd.
> Some to the fascination of a name,

111

Surrender judgment hood-wink'd. Some the style
Infatuates, and through labyrinths and wilds
Of error leads them, by a tune entranced.
While sloth seduces more, too weak to bear
The insupportable fatigue of thought,
And swallowing, therefore, without pause or choice,
The total grist unsifted, husks and all.

—*The Task, 6.98–108*

People buy books for different reasons—they like the author, something about the jacket or title appeals to them, someone recommended they read a particular book. But as with all the other products of human culture, there is the danger that books might lead people "through labyrinths and wilds / Of error." Books, after all, promote ideas, using a widely available cultural form to advertise whatever the author and publisher may agree will be of sufficient interest to enough readers to allow the publishing house to turn a profit. Thus we should expect bookstores to have plenty to say to us about the interests and concerns of people, and the kinds of ideas they find appealing or helpful.

Job did not have bookstores to prompt him to think about such matters; indeed, he did not even have books! But his perception and experience of cultural artifacts, such as a judge seeking to reconcile alienated parties, or the work of his own hands, clearly seem to have prompted him to theological considerations. Might not a bookstore do the same for us? While not as commonplace as trees, bookstores are at least as interesting. Certainly a great many trees have been fruitfully employed in the construction of bookstores and the shelves of paper they display. And like trees, bookstores can reveal much to us about the knowledge of God, and about the knowledge of God of those who frequent such establishments.

A place serious about books. Walk into the secular bookstore in my community—one of the large chain stores cropping up all over the land—and you are immediately impressed with the idea that this store is *serious* about books. The wood panels, bright lights, handsome chairs distributed throughout, expensive wooden shelves, and scores of thousands of books open up a world of serious reading, leisurely contemplation, and lavish literary self-indulgence. Books of every kind, dealing with virtually every subject, line the shelves. As I walk through the store I pay attention to the proportionality of spacing. There are more books of contemporary fiction than any other sort, followed by a neck-and-neck competition between self-help books, books about money and business, and how-to books dealing with everything from cooking to woodworking. The smallest sections include books about philosophy, education, and music. The section of religious books offers titles from just about every world religion, and is larger overall than the last three mentioned sections combined. There are more books about Christianity in this section than about all other religions taken together. I notice that people are fairly evenly distributed throughout the store, browsing books in practically every section (although on this day the section of art books looks like a wallflower at a seventh-grade dance). The magazine kiosk takes up almost an entire wall, with hundreds of different magazines to offer. Very few of the titles displayed would appeal to researchers or academics, however. Most of the magazines are of a distinctly popular sort. The café features an assortment of coffees and refreshments and displays a large mural of several well-known writers sitting together at a café. The suggestion is not subtle: bring your books, have a cup of coffee, and join in the fellowship of serious readers, writers, and thinkers. As I move toward the checkout counter, I become aware of a number of items that are not books—leather book covers, calendars, puzzles, chocolates and mints, mugs, T-shirts, pens, and so forth. These are largely "impulse items," designed to appeal to the sense of "Oh, why not?" that shoppers often succumb to as they stand in line waiting to buy their books.

God and His truth in the bookstore. How might such an experience enhance our knowledge of God? Certainly it reminds us that our contemporaries put a great deal of stock in the promise of knowledge, and that they are devoted to maximizing every opportunity for the workings of capitalist economics. Each of these observations might be further explored as to what they tell us about the divine economy and the

113

idols of our secular age. I want to focus on only two of many lessons to be gained from our visit.

First, for all their secularity, contemporary, postmodern people cannot rid themselves of the knowledge of God. A bookstore such as this illustrates in unmistakable ways what Paul describes in Romans 1:18–32. God is ever-present and working to make Himself known to men and women through created things—in this case, a bookstore. And He is present not only in the religious section, but in many of the other sections of the store as well. Indeed, among the most popular sections in my local bookstore are the shelves holding books on "New Age" religions, where perversions of the true knowledge of God are eagerly perused. Religious books are featured prominently in various sections, and they appear to be holding their own against most other types of books at the checkout counter. Postmodern people, it seems, cannot get away from God. He continues to call out to them, to remind them of His existence, and to summon them to consider Him. Like the natural world, constantly testifying to the divinity and power of God, a secular bookstore heralds His voice in nearly every section. The vast majority of men and women in our society prefer not to seek the Lord but turn instead to other interests, ignoring the wooing of God's Spirit as they devote themselves to more self-indulgent concerns. And yet He is there, just as He is throughout the creation, sending out His line and calling people to consider and seek Him while He may be found.

With the rise of Christian bookstores, we might suppose that proprietors of secular bookstores would be happy to relinquish that special interest to such establishments. Yet the shelves of Christian books persist in secular bookstores, as do those of many other religions, not only in the section designated for religious writings but throughout the store as well. No reputable modern bookstore would be without a religious section, or the many Christian books that dominate that section, for to do so would be to ignore not only a significant business market, but also that which in a more profound way speaks of an abiding awareness from which no generation can completely escape.

The trade in secular books mirrors the natural world in that it offers the line from God to every customer. Just as He is declaring His glory through the trees, He is making His presence known through these handsome by-products of that wondrous work of nature. A trip to a bookstore can remind us that, for all their apparent secularity and indifference to matters religious, people are still open to conversing about spiritual matters. This should encourage us in our work of evangelism to get to know people better, to discover their interests and concerns, and to learn how to engage them in meaningful conversations, so that we can speak the Word of God in ways they will be more likely to hear (1 Cor. 9:19–23).

The second observation is related to the first. Today's large bookstores help us to understand the "idols" to which our contemporaries are turning instead of worshiping and serving the living God. A casual glance at the list of bestsellers on the special shelf at the bookstore discloses the principal deities of the secular pantheon. Chief among them are various kinds of escapism (such as fiction provides), idols of wealth and health, and the gods of sport, entertainment, and sex. These are the books to which most people in secular bookstores are turning, gladly sacrificing their wealth and time to submit to the wisdom of their chosen deity. Here they seek new hope, grovel before the latest diet or plan for success, or consult for wisdom in daily life—all in a vain hope to discover meaning, happiness, and purpose. The annual proliferation of new titles in these sections, and the success of many of these titles, suggests that, like the ancient Athenians to whom Paul proclaimed the gospel, postmodern people are in constant pursuit of some new experience, thrill, or edge to provide them the satisfaction they seek. The idols to which our contemporaries appeal for a full and happy life satisfy only for a season, and must be regularly reinforced or replaced. The hearts of our contemporaries are restless, but they will find no rest in the false idols of a secular age. More likely, they will be "hood-wink'd" into some temporary thrill, unworkable scheme, or hopeless fantasy. They will be back for the next installment or bestseller in no time.

By observing the culture represented in a secular bookstore—its décor, offerings, and presentation—we may learn a great deal about the persistence of God and the theology by which our postmodern contemporaries seek to make sense out of their lives. But there is more to discover of a decidedly theological nature from our visit to a bookstore, which we can discern by a more careful observation of two people we encounter on our visit.

Once upon a time in the bookstore. In growing frustration, Job asked his tormentors, "Hast thou eyes of flesh? or seest thou as man seeth?" (Job 10:4). Job was not impressed by the superficial analyses his friends were proffering of his desperate situation. He wanted to know what God thought, how God would explain this situation. His friends were looking merely to outward things and circumstances; they could not see into Job's heart, which, he continually protested, was pure and upright before the Lord. God told Samuel that men are too easily satisfied with the merely superficial in life, and are easily impressed by appearances (1 Sam. 16:7). During my visit to the bookstore, this profound theological truth was reinforced in what to me was a sad encounter with two teenage girls.

I had purchased a coffee and found a table near the railing in the elevated café, just to relax and think a little. Before long, two girls barely into their teens plopped down on the cushy seats just beneath me and plunked a stack of women's magazines down on the table between them. I could read a few of the titles, but they seemed hardly the kinds of magazines that these girls' parents might have purchased for them. Indeed, no parents were in sight, so I suspected that these kids had conspired together for an afternoon of naughtiness. Giggling and shushing one another, they dived into the stack. I could not see what they were reading or the pictures they were studying, but their faces and reactions told me everything I needed to know.

One girl clutched a full-page photo to her breast, threw her head back, and sighed, "Too cool!" before she shoved the picture in front of her friend for examination. Together they smoothed the palms of their hands over the photo with obvious delight. Then back to their individual reading. Shortly, the other girl, enthralled with something obviously illicit, let her mouth fall open, covered it with her hand, and muttered, "Oh, my God!" before bursting into uncontrolled giggling. Her friend came over to see what had caused this reaction, and the amazed girl eagerly, though barely audibly, read the text that had elicited her response. Her friend collapsed in a mock swoon on the floor. After a while they took to looking at ads, remarking on colors of makeup, hairstyles, models' clothing and jewelry, and so forth, their eyes wide with fond hopes and daring dreams. Sighs, whines, gushes, and drools abounded. This went on for nearly an hour; then, almost as if they had received some common internal signal, they got up and left, leaving the magazines to languish on the table.

My immediate response was, "Man looks on outward things." What else might these two girls have done with that time? Whatever it might have been, they chose to fill the hour nurturing their vision of the good life, the life of beauty, luxury, and sensuality, indulging their lusts with abandon as they thumbed the pages of those women's magazines. What are we teaching our children? I thought, as I reflected on what I had observed. What dreams do we encourage in them? What longings and aspirations? What do we hold out to them as of value and significance for full and abundant life? Are we abandoning them to the Molech of pop culture and the false idols of unending beauty and perfect happiness? Certainly the editors of those magazines have a vision of what really matters in life, and they are devoted to their own ideas about what is beautiful, good, and true, eagerly marketing those ideas to like-minded readers. Success, happiness, and a life worth living, they would have those two children believe, consists in being beautiful, having it all, realizing your fantasies, and continually enjoying more and more of the same. The idols of our material, sensual age are ferociously promoted through the popular media, to which young children have all-too-ready access. They learn early how they ought to think about what's really important and are then reinforced in those ideas throughout their lives.

But what about those who don't measure up? Who will never be beautiful or rich? Whose husbands or boyfriends don't look at all like the latest rock or film idol? And who will spend their lives envious, jealous, resentful, frustrated, and disillusioned? Or who watch helplessly as beauty fades, riches fail to satisfy, and husbands run off with the next young thing who makes their hearts twitter? Or what of those, perhaps more homely and retiring, who seek inner beauty and dream of literary prizes, a home full of children, or service to God in some

117

distant land? What do the editors of these magazines have to say to them? Losers!

Their message is powerful and persuasive, and they have become expertly adept at coaxing hard-earned money from wannabes of every age who have bought their line about what really matters in life. But their line is not true. While our contemporaries are busy looking on the outward person, they are neglecting the matters of the heart that God is continuously inspecting and by which we will all stand or fall before Him. As I felt my anger growing toward the promulgators of pop culture and its lies of self-indulgence and sensuality, I was rebuked that we in the Christian community, who hold the truth of God in the vessels of flesh, are not more aggressive in making that truth known. Why are we not able to present the Christian life to young people in more compelling and convincing terms? Indeed, why do we so readily sacrifice our own children to the Molech of pop culture? Why do we go along with every cultural trend or fad without carefully analyzing its message or considering how it may distract us from seeking the kingdom of God? Must it always be true that the children of this unbelieving age are wiser in their generation than the children of light (Luke 16:8)?

As I sat stewing in my coffee, I could only give thanks to God for tearing away the scales that had once blinded my eyes to truth, and asked forgiveness for my own failure to be more active in spreading the good news of Jesus. I had been reminded of the blindness of sin, the allure of material and sensual idols, the subterfuge of pop culture, and the failure of the church to proclaim and embody a new vision of the full and abundant life. I quickly made some notes about this experience and later, in order to firm up my impressions and create a memorial of my observations to remind me of at least some of what I believe God had shown me through those two young girls, wrote the following sonnet:

Two Young Girls at the Bookstore

> A stack of women's magazines provides
> their afternoon diversion. They would learn
> to be more beautiful, or how to earn

118

more money, or the hot new fashions brides
will be attired in for the season, besides
the latest word on better sex. By turns,
they read and laugh and sigh and gawk and yearn
to be more grown-up, like the greedy guides

who prey upon their trust and lead them to
believe that sexy, rich, and lavish are
the norms in life, that it's every woman's right
to all that glitters, and that those who do
not manage to achieve these ends debar
themselves from happiness to a lesser plight.

Each time I read that sonnet, I relive that experience—to my sadness
and shame, but great gratitude.

"That I Might Receive My Sight"

How often the Scriptures urge us to use our senses to perceive and
experience the goodness, greatness, and mercy of God, and to learn
something of how we should relate to Him. Sparrows, lilies, mountains, rivers; coins, fallen towers, millstones; people marrying, bury-
ing their dead, or paying their alms; sounds, tastes, and all manner of
sensations—all these and much, much more offer us the opportunity
for precious insights into the ways and will of God. But we are too
busy, too much in a hurry, or too distracted by the mundaneness of it
all to think more deeply about what God may be trying to say to us.
The promise of creational theology is that by learning to perceive and
experience creation, culture, and the actions of conscience with greater
care and consistency, we might enter more fully into the knowledge of
God, and grow in a more worshipful relationship with Him. As Scott
Hoezee puts it,

we need to stop our busy lives long enough to peer out into the world;
stop long enough to stare into tide pools and forests to see what is really
there. The longer you look and the closer you pay attention, the more

119

you will see. And the more you see, the better poised you will be to give intelligent, informed, pointed praise to the Creator for all the specific wonders he has made.[16]

But we, like Job, must make a covenant with our eyes to seek the revelation of God in creation, observing carefully, reflecting deeply, and searching the Scriptures for light from God on how best to understand the things we have seen. Let ours be the prayer of that blind man who, when asked by Jesus what he would have the Savior do for him, replied, "Lord, that I might receive my sight" (Mark 10:51). Moments of careful observing may result in rewarding insights as we take up the happy task of creational theology, bent on seeking the Lord and discerning His line in the things He has made, until He shows Himself and His truth to us in flashes of sudden insight or by gradual illumination:

> In that blest moment, Nature, throwing wide
> Her veil opake, discloses with a smile
> The Author of her beauties, who, retired
> Behind his own creation, works unseen
> By the impure, and hears his power denied:
> Thou art the source and center of all minds,
> Their only point of rest, eternal Word!
>
> —*The Task*, 5.891–97

The challenge of observing general revelation by means of creational theology is laden with excitement. What vistas of glory are waiting to be discovered! What powerful tools of worship, mutual encouragement and edification, culture-building, and evangelism lie within our grasp! By taking up the challenge of creational theology, we will find that our knowledge of God is deepened, our sense of His presence inestimably enlarged, our joy in knowing His steadfast love abundantly magnified, our confidence in His power greatly increased, and our visibility as a distinct community, with a clear and compelling worldview and a culture and ethic to match, gloriously heightened.

Our greatest need in this task is for exemplars and practitioners to guide us, to take us by the hand and lead us up the forbidding slopes

120

of the mountain of general revelation. Step by step, through the disciplines of creational theology, we will then ascend to greater heights of the knowledge of God. And several such exemplars and practitioners are readily at hand, chief among them Jonathan Edwards.

Questions for Study or Discussion

1. Why does it seem to make sense to refer to the discipline outlined in this chapter by the term "creational theology"? How does this term differ from "natural theology"?

2. Review the eight presuppositions of creational theology outlined above. Which, if any, are new to your thinking? How do these presuppositions challenge your thinking about the area of general revelation?

3. Why do you think so few Christians seem to be involved in creational theology? How has the notion of "scholarly objectivity" affected the practice of creational theology?

4. Do any particular aspects of the discipline of creational theology disturb you? Challenge you? Give you pause? Excite your imagination? Explain.

5. What might it look like if you started doing creational theology? What kinds of things would be involved?

The Happy Task of Creational Theology

Activity 4

Before going on to the next chapter, make at least three new entries in your notebook—one each from the areas of creation, culture, and the actions of conscience. Summarize your observations, how you reacted and felt, what thoughts went through your mind, and what, if any, teachings or passages of Scripture you recalled. Choose one of those observations and devote at least an hour to meditating on it. Ask yourself specifically:

- What does this experience suggest about God? About His beauty, goodness, or truth? About the human condition as Scripture proclaims it?
- How does this experience help you to understand more completely—with heart as well as mind—the teaching of Scripture from any of the passages you have noted?
- End this exercise with an extended season of praise to God for what He has shown you of Himself.
- Meet with your conversation partner and share your observations and meditations.

PART 3

JONATHAN EDWARDS ON GENERAL REVELATION AND CREATIONAL THEOLOGY

Mountain Mists
Below Cheat Mountain
Elkins, West Virginia

I understand what led the Greeks to think
their gods inhabited the mountain heights.
For when the morning mists crawl through the trees

these summery days, their fingers reaching down
toward the earth below, I wonder what's
impelling them, compelling them to bend

so low, only to draw back once again. Just what
do they conceal within their vapors? Is
the Deity Himself, as those old Greeks

believed, ensconced among those clouds, and might
a mortal such as I rise up and greet
Him there, be taken up to meet Him there?

5

JONATHAN EDWARDS
AND GENERAL REVELATION

*And I gave my heart to seek and search out by wisdom
concerning all things that are done under heaven . . .*
—Ecclesiastes 1:13

*And it is farther to be considered, that what God aimed
at in the creation of the world, as the end which he had
ultimately in view, was that communication of himself
which he intended through all eternity.*
—Jonathan Edwards[1]

'Tis born with all: the love of Nature's works
Is an ingredient in the compound man,
Infused at the creation of the kind.
And, though the Almighty Maker has throughout
Discriminated each from each, by strokes
And touches of his hand, with so much art
Diversified, that two were never found
Twins at all points—yet this obtains in all,
That all discern a beauty in his works,
And all can taste them . . .

—*The Task*, 4.731–40

We would expect Jonathan Edwards, as a theologian in the Reformed tradition, to endorse the doctrine of general revelation as it had been developed by his theological forebears, especially John Calvin and the Westminster divines. But it might surprise us to find, as we do in Edwards's works, such an extensive and varied use of this doctrine in the work of the gospel. For Jonathan Edwards, the doctrine of general revelation was as much a tool in his gospel armamentarium as any other of the heads of doctrine to which he so consistently and passionately appealed in his preaching. That God was revealing Himself in the things He had made, making something of Himself, His purposes, and His ways known for all to see, was for Edwards a tool to be used in the work of the kingdom, a precision instrument to be applied with great energy and skill to the particular tasks for which the Giver of all truth intended it. Edwards believed indeed that it is "an ingredient in the compound of man" to "discern a beauty in his works," and he made more of this general revelation than any theologian before or since.

Edwards is, thus, no minimizer of this important doctrine; nor, as we will see, does he fall into the snare of those Roman Catholic and evangelical maximizers who put more trust in general revelation than is warranted by the teaching of Scripture. Instead, Edwards plowed new ground with the doctrine of general revelation, wielding it with mighty force against both lost and saved according to his peculiar understanding of how that doctrine might be used for the purposes of the gospel. He earnestly believed that God's revelation in creation could have powerful effects on all men, but especially on those with whom God's Spirit was striving in order to bring them to Himself, as well as those who had already come into a saving relationship with Him through Jesus Christ. As we will see, it is in his careful and consistent use of the doctrine of general revelation that the creational theology of Jonathan Edwards emerges for our consideration.

Edwards on General Revelation

Let us allow Edwards to speak for himself on the subject of general revelation. His words reflect a clear understanding and unswerving commitment to the teaching of Scripture and the Reformed tradition on this subject. We can discern his fundamental conviction concerning this doctrine in the quote with which this chapter begins: God fully intended that all He made should communicate something of Himself. Edwards continues:

> There are many reasons to think that what God has in view, in an increasing communication of himself through eternity, is an *increasing* knowledge of God, love to him, and joy in him. And it is to be considered, that the more those divine communications *increase* in the creature, the more it becomes one with God: for so much the more is it united to God in love, the heart is drawn nearer and nearer to God, and the union with him becomes more firm and close: and, at the same time, the creature becomes more and more *conformed* to God.[2]

Edwards No Maximizer

Already Edwards should be raising questions in our minds, since it might appear from this quotation in one of his most important works that Edwards is in danger of falling into the snare of the maximizers of the doctrine of general revelation. He plainly says that God intends through the revelation of Himself in creation that those creatures capable of discerning Him thereby should increase in knowledge of Him. Moreover, the knowledge of God that His image-bearers are able to discern in the things He has made should lead them to greater love for Him, and to increasing conformity to His image as they are ever more deeply renewed in knowledge of Him through what He has made. This sounds like natural religion, like those who insist that the revelation of God in nature is sufficient to bring them to a true knowledge of God, which can then lead quite naturally and easily to accepting the claims of Christ and entering into salvation.

But let's not get ahead of Edwards, nor read into this statement more than is justified. In fact, Edwards does believe precisely what he says, and what I have outlined above. But he holds these convictions with some serious qualifications, as we will see.

What We May Learn from General Revelation

In a sermon on Psalm 46:10, Edwards outlines the broad parameters of what we may expect to learn about God from what He is revealing of Himself in the creation:

> It is most evident by the works of God, that his understanding and power are infinite; for he that hath made all things out of nothing, and upholds, and governs, and manages all things every moment, in all ages, without growing weary, must be of infinite power. He must also be of infinite knowledge; for if he made all things, and upholds and governs all things continually, it will follow, that he knows and perfectly sees all things, great and small, in heaven and earth, continually at one view . . . Being thus infinite in understanding and power, he must also be perfectly holy . . .[3]

Besides giving clear evidence of His existence, God's works reveal His wisdom and power, showing that He is both omnipotent and omniscient, and leading to the conclusion that He is perfectly holy. Being omnipotent and omniscient, God must also necessarily be holy, according to Edwards. As we study the works of His hands, we should expect further illumination to fill our minds and stir our affections concerning the power, wisdom, and holiness of God. These attributes God reveals in His Word; the study of general revelation can further illuminate these concepts, making them more real to our minds, more potent in our affections, and more powerful to change our lives.

God's Revelation Continuous: Response to Deism

We should be sure to notice the great emphasis that Edwards puts on God's continuous attention to His creation—"every moment," "all ages," "without growing weary," and so forth. Edwards is keeping in mind the Deists, who taught that God stood aloof from His creation, having invested it with sufficient laws, inherent powers, and unchanging structure so that it manages and sustains itself. William Cowper also mocked the folly and pretensions of such deistic thinking in a typically Reformed and biblical manner:

Some say that in the origin of things,
When all creation started into birth,
The infant elements received a law
From which they swerved not since. That under force
Of that controlling ordinance they move,
And heed not His immediate hand who first
Prescribed their course, to regulate it now.
Thus dream they, and contrive to save a God
The remembrance of his own concerns, and spare
The great Artificer of all that moves
The stress of a continual act, the pain
Of unremitted vigilance and care,
As too laborious and severe a task.
So man, the moth, is not afraid, it seems,
To span omnipotence, and measure might
That knows no measure, by the scanty rule
And standard of his own, that is to-day,
And is not ere to-morrow's sun go down.
But how should matter occupy a charge,
Dull as it is, and satisfy a law
So vast in its demands, unless impell'd
To ceaseless service by a ceaseless force,
And under pressure of some conscious cause?
The Lord of all, himself through all diffused,
Sustains, and is the life of all that lives.

—*The Task,* 5.198–222

Cowper, with Edwards, saw a continuous presence of God in the things He has made. He does not need to be spared "the stress of a continual act" of upholding, directing, and sustaining all things.

The Effects of the Fall

Then why, we might wonder, do so few people, whether lost or saved, seem to take note of God's glory in general revelation? Preaching on Psalm 94:8–11, Edwards divorced himself from the error of the maximizers of the doctrine of general revelation by showing that he

129

understood how sinful men have distorted the revelation of God in creation:

> Man has faculties given him whereby he is well capable of inferring the being of the Creator from the creatures. The invisible things of God are very plainly and clearly to be seen by the things that are made; and the perfections of the Divine Being, his eternal power and Godhead, are very manifest in the works of his hands. And yet grossly absurd notions concerning the Godhead have prevailed in the world. Instead of acknowledging and worshipping the *true* God, they have fallen off to the worship of idols. Instead of acknowledging the *one* only true God, they have made a *multitude* of deities. Instead of worshipping a God, who is an almighty, infinite, all-wise, and holy Spirit, they have worshipped the hosts of heaven, the sun, moon, and stars; and the works of their own hands, images of gold and silver, brass and iron, wood and stone; gods that can neither hear, nor see, nor walk, nor speak, nor do, nor know any thing.[4]

God's revelation in the things He has made is exceedingly clear, and all men have the ability to discern what He is revealing of Himself. Yet they do not; instead, they fashion gods according to their own thinking, false and useless deities, and fall down and worship them. Thus they reject the knowledge of God and head off on a course of idolatry and self-destruction. Edwards adds, to emphasize his point of man's ignorance:

> Natural men of the greatest abilities and learning, are as ignorant [of the knowledge of God] as the weakest and most unlearned; yea, as ignorant as the very stocks and stones; for they see, and can see nothing of it at all.[5]

No amount of sophisticated learning can rescue man from his ignorance of the knowledge of God that He is revealing through the creation. That is because man, in his natural estate, is blinded to that revelation, though it is ever so clear and compelling. Even his most careful and powerful reasoning, improved and enlarged over generations, cannot lead man to the knowledge of God on the basis of general revelation alone:

130

What instance can be mentioned, from any history, of any one nation under the sun, that emerged from atheism or idolatry, into the knowledge or adoration of the one true God, without the assistance of revelation? The Americans, the Africans, the Tartars, and ingenious Chinese, have had time enough, one would think, to find out the true and right idea of God; and yet, after above five thousand years' improvements, and the full exercise of reason, they have, at this day, got no further in their progress towards the true religion, than to the worship of sticks and stones and devils. How many thousand years must be allowed to these nations, to reason themselves into the true religion? What the light of nature and reason could do to investigate the knowledge of God, is best seen by what they have already done. We cannot argue more convincingly on any foundation, than that of known and incontestable facts.[6]

Natural man, blinded by sin, will never reason himself into the true knowledge of God. That, Edwards maintains, can be achieved only through the special revelation that God makes of Himself in Scripture and Jesus Christ. The gospel and the preaching of it are alone sufficient to lead men to the knowledge and love of God, which is salvation.

Edwards on General Revelation: A Summary Thus Far

This brief sampler of Edwards's words on general revelation is typical of what we find in other places in his works. Let's try for a summary from just this much of Edwards concerning his views of the doctrine of general revelation. His conclusions reflect what we have already seen from Scripture and the Reformed tradition:

1. God is clearly revealing Himself in the things He has made, manifesting His wisdom, power, and deity.
2. Men possess faculties sufficient to lead them to know the Lord, and in fact, they all do know Him at some level.
3. Yet men in their natural estate will not acknowledge what they see of God, will not enter into the knowledge of Him, will not love and serve Him; instead, they turn to idols of their own construction as their devotional outlet.

131

4. As a result, natural men fall under the wrath of God and are in danger of His eternal judgment.

Men will be rescued from this tragic situation only when they have been enlightened by the gospel of Jesus Christ. Thus, it is a testimony to God's great mercy that He has sent His Son into the world for the salvation of ungrateful, rebellious, blind, and lost sinners:

> This doctrine should make us sensible, how great a *mercy* it is to mankind, that God has sent his own Son into the world, to be the *light* of the world . . . He has sent him to be the light of the world, as he says of himself, "I am come a light into the world." When he came, he brought glorious light. It was like the day-spring from on high, visiting a dark world . . . Though mankind be fallen into such darkness, and the world be mostly in the kingdom of darkness; yet the Scripture often speaks of a *glorious day*, wherein light shall fill the earth . . . When this shall be accomplished, it will be by a *remarkable pouring out of God's own Spirit, with the plain preaching of the gospel of his Son*; the preaching of the spiritual, mysterious doctrines of Christ crucified, which to the learned men of this world are foolishness; those doctrines, which are *the stumbling-block of this learned age* . . . It will not be by the enticing words of man's wisdom; but by the demonstration of the Spirit, and of power. Not by the wisdom of this world, nor by the princes of this world, that come to nought: but by the gospel, that contains the wisdom of God in a mystery, even the hidden wisdom, which none of the princes of this world, who have nothing to enlighten them but their own learning, know any thing of.[7]

Thus, it would seem that any and all appeals to general revelation would be a waste of time, even a rejection of the teaching of Scripture concerning the way of salvation. We would be best served, in reaching lost men, to avoid all such appeals, for they have the effect only of leading them further and further into ignorance and rebellion. We might think that we should simply preach the gospel to them, and preach it over and over again, until the Spirit of God is pleased to give them enlightenment and bring them to the true knowledge of God.

Edwards No Minimizer

Edwards would thus seem to count himself among the minimizers of the doctrine of general revelation, those who contend that there is such a revelation but that appealing to it is useless. Except for this one thing: Edwards's works are filled with careful, elaborate, detailed, and impassioned appeals to the revelation of God in creation! How do we account for this? Edwards unequivocally denies the sufficiency of general revelation to lead men to the true knowledge of God. Yet he makes extensive, detailed, and multifaceted use of general revelation as part of his labors in the gospel. Is he merely inconsistent with himself? Careless in his doctrine? Hardly. As we will see, Edwards makes use of the doctrine of general revelation in a framework of creational theology that understands God's revelation in creation for what it is and embraces and employs it according to God's own intentions in the progress of the gospel and the furthering of His kingdom.

Gerstner on Edwards's Understanding of General Revelation

The Reformed community, and Christians in general, will forever be in the debt of the late Dr. John Gerstner, who devoted much of his theological career to reviving interest in the works of Jonathan Edwards and encouraging the reading, study, and use of Edwards's extensive corpus in the disciplined pursuit of the knowledge of God. There is hardly an aspect of Edwards's theology that Dr. Gerstner did not labor to explain, either in his classes and public lectures or in his many works. Gerstner provides a most helpful summary of Edwards's approach to the doctrine of general revelation in his magnum opus, *The Rational Biblical Theology of Jonathan Edwards*. Gerstner notes thirteen aspects to Edwards's view of this subject:

1. Light comes into the mind of man.
2. Unregenerate man being a sinner and naturally a hater of light tries to get rid of this unwelcome light which he cannot avoid.
3. Thus he tries to bury it out of his sight.

133

4. This angers God who is light and He punishes man by letting him go his way in darkness.

5. Man in his hatred and under divine punishment tries to explain away that light that he has seen and suppresses.

6. God lets him go ever deeper into his self-made darkness and the most brilliant thinkers become the most darkened in understanding, the devil himself being the "greatest blockhead of all" according to Edwards.

7. Then God gives special divine revelation.

8. Revelation is met with even greater opposition from unregenerate men because it is so much brighter light which he therefore hates more.

9. At some point, God changes the disposition of the elect from one hating light to one loving it.

10. Then all the suppressed light comes welcome to the surface of conscious experience and expression and with it a desire for ever greater light.

11. Converted men even grow in the light of nature. They revel in the light of special revelation. They now love light—all light.

12. Then the natural revelation which was always there and always compelling but always suppressed and always denied comes into free and happy acknowledgement.

13. So if men are not converted they will suppress the light they have and attempt to deny it.[8]

Two Observations

Let us make a couple of observations concerning Gerstner's summary.

1. We recognize here in his summary of Edwards the broad parameters of the Reformed doctrine of general revelation: there is such revelation; men can see it; but they are willfully blind to it. Only the light of special revelation can open their eyes to the true knowledge of God, including that which is coming through general revelation. Edwards, as we have seen, was well within the tradition of Reformed thinkers on this important doctrine.

2. But Gerstner rightly discerns in Edwards's thinking two signifi-cant improvements in the Reformed doctrine of general revelation as we have been considering it thus far.

First, Gerstner shows that exposure to the light of special revela-tion will begin to have an effect on the elect of God, even as they con-tinue in an unregenerate state, such that they begin to be more open to any and all revelation of God (points 7 and 9). As the elect are exposed to the Word of God, and the gospel of Jesus Christ as the heart of that Word, God begins to work so that fissures are created in their hardened hearts. Through these the light of general revelation can begin to filter through and make way for the clearer, brighter light of special revelation (points 9 and 10). At point 7 Edwards, according to Gerstner, is not saying that God converts the elect, at least not at this stage; rather, he means simply that He brings the light of special rev-elation to bear against them. The process of the effectual calling of the elect begins at this point and may continue for some time. Only at point 9 does effectual calling begin to do the work that eventuates in the new birth. As we know from Edwards's writings, the new birth may be quite sudden and dramatic, or it may be the result of a long period during which a person is drawn to acknowledge the truth of Scripture and the gospel. But the *process* of God's effectually calling His elect unto Himself apparently, according to Edwards, includes and can be aided by appeals to general revelation.

Meanwhile, the unregenerate nonelect, in the face of special reve-lation, respond by hating that light from God even more than they do the light of creation, for it is so much brighter and clearer (point 8). The nonelect harden their hearts further. So as the light of special rev-elation and the gospel is added to that of creation, two processes are at work at the same time, one wooing and drawing the elect to a sav-ing knowledge of God, and one hardening the nonelect even more than previously. Both of these processes are confirmations of the teaching of God's Word. Under the light of Scripture and the call of the gospel, some people gradually begin to view general revelation with more sym-pathetic eyes, while others are hardened more and more. This, at least, is what Edwards believed and what his practice reflects, as we will see. His views support the presuppositions that we previously outlined concerning the use of creational theology in approaching the field of general revelation.

Edwards's use of general revelation thus differs from the natural theology of some Christian apologists in ways that we will explain and illustrate in more detail in a subsequent chapter. Reformed theology, with its doctrine of election, can explain why some people seem to "get the point"—at least to a certain extent—of general revelation and begin to warm to it, while others merely continue to shrug off the evidence of God's self-disclosures in the creation and seem to become even more hardened to God's truth. Thus, Reformed theologians such as Edwards can provide adequate justification for the use of general revelation in the work of the gospel without falling into contradiction or inconsistency. They are neither maximizers nor minimizers of this doctrine. As we will see, Edwards justified his own use of general revelation on the basis of the effectual striving of God's Spirit with those whom God had chosen and was calling to Himself.

Second, Gerstner points out that Edwards, certainly by his own example, but also in his teaching, insists that once God has begun to call an elect sinner to a saving knowledge of Himself through the gospel of Jesus Christ, all the previous light received by the person from God via general revelation begins to make sense (points 9 and 10). Cowper saw the same thing, as he wrote concerning astronomy, philosophy, and other branches of learning:

> But never yet did philosophic tube,
> That brings the planets home into the eye
> Of observation, and discovers, else
> Not visible, his family of worlds,
> Discover Him that rules them: such a veil
> Hangs over mortal eyes, blind from the birth,
> And dark in things divine. Full often too,
> Our wayward intellect, the more we learn
> Of nature, overlooks her Author more,
> From instrumental causes proud to draw
> Conclusions retrograde and mad mistake.
> But if his word once teach us,—shoot a ray
> Through all the heart's dark chambers, and reveal

136

Truths undiscern'd but by that holy light,
Then all is plain. Philosophy, baptized
In the pure fountain of eternal love,
Has eyes indeed; and viewing all she sees
As meant to indicate a God to man,
Gives *Him* his praise, and forfeits not her own.

—The Task, 3.229–47

Once the light of Scripture and the gospel have begun to open their eyes, the redeemed of the Lord start to love God's light, wherever it can be found and as much as they can discover, because it leads them to an ever-deepening relationship with God and brings them increasingly into conformity with His image (points 10–12). Discovering themselves to be creatures of a merciful and compassionate Creator, who sent His Son for their redemption, they, in gratitude, eagerly seek out the knowledge of God in the revelation of His Word and in general revelation. With respect to the latter, no longer are God's redeemed ones condemned to flounder in the ignorance and uncertainties of "natural revelation"; now they can see general revelation for what it is. They recognize that the creation is one vast book of the world, a voluminous revelation of God. Guided by the light of Scripture and the gospel, they can begin to "read" that book for what it has to say about God and how it can benefit their walk with Him. Now they can think back on all the ways in which God has been speaking to them in the past through the things He has made. And now they can begin to delight in His works, study them, and by the light of creation, illuminated by Scripture and gospel, grow in the grace and knowledge of the Lord.

They can begin, in short, to do creational theology.

Edwards thus gives us strong encouragement to take seriously the revelation of God in creation, culture, and the conscience of man. God is at work here, making Himself known and drawing His own ever more closely to Himself. He illuminates His glory in the creation by His Spirit, working with His Word, and ignites in the hearts of those who have come to know Him a greater zeal for seeking the light and truth of God wherever it may be found. Thus, in his understanding of

137

the doctrine of general revelation, Edwards provides sound encouragement for us to proceed on to the work of creational theology. And in his practice, as we will see, he points the way along a wondrous and luminous path, all too frequently ignored and not taken.

Questions for Study or Discussion

1. How can we see that Edwards is typical of Reformed theologians in his understanding of general revelation? In what ways does he improve on Calvin and the Westminster divines in this area?

2. Can you indict Edwards as either a minimizer or a maximizer of general revelation? Explain.

3. How did Edwards understand general and special revelation to work on God's elect? On the reprobate? On the redeemed? What relationship between general and special revelation does Edwards recommend?

4. Is there a difference between seeing the world as "nature" or "natural" and seeing it as "creation" or "created"? What is the difference? How does the difference reflect the theological perspective of those who use either term? Which should a biblical Christian prefer? Why?

5. Do you feel as though you are beginning to realize the goals you set for yourself at the end of the last chapter? In what ways?

The Happy Task of Creational Theology

Activity 5

Spend an hour or so reviewing all the entries you have made in your notebook. On a separate sheet, write a few paragraphs concerning what you have observed about the wisdom, power, and holiness of God in these aspects of His general revelation. Share your conclusions with your conversation partner. Ask yourself how you might use these observations when you are explaining the gospel to a lost friend.

6

Jonathan Edwards and Creational Theology

He hath made every thing beautiful in his time: also he hath set the world in their heart, so that no man can find out the work that God maketh from the beginning to the end.
—Ecclesiastes 3:11

Man was created to praise, reverence, and serve God our Lord, and thereby to save his soul. And the other things on the face of the earth were created for man's sake, and to help him in the following out of the end for which he was created . . . any day, any minute we bless God for our being or for anything, for food, for sunlight, we do and are what we are meant for, made for—things that give and mean to give glory to God. This is a thing to live for. Then make haste so to live.
—Gerard Manley Hopkins[1]

We are now ready to take a more detailed look at various ways in which Jonathan Edwards made use of the doctrine of general revelation according to a creational-theology mode such as was outlined and

139

illustrated in chapter 4. As we have seen, Edwards's view of general revelation is thoroughly biblical and Reformed: There is revelation from God in the things He has made, given to lead men to know and glorify Him. That revelation is clear and compelling, giving us insight into the wisdom, power, and holiness of God. Sinful men will not receive it; they are thus under His wrath. Yet the elect of God will be drawn by the light of general revelation, in the context of the preaching of the gospel, and be strengthened in their faith by it after coming to saving knowledge of Christ.

Even though sinful men will not see God in the revelation He gives them through the creation, Edwards, throughout the course of his ministry, appealed to his congregation (many of whom he regarded as unsaved) to consider what God was saying to them through general revelation. Yet for the most part, he made use of general revelation in the context of the Word of God and the gospel. And he appealed to it fervently because he believed that, working with the gospel, the Spirit of God would use such revelation to strive with the elect and draw them on toward the true knowledge of God in Christ. Edwards, like Hopkins, understood that men were created to know and glorify God, and as part of his effort to help his congregation to realize that end, he turned to God's general revelation.

All the examples we will consider in this chapter are used in Edwards's preaching and writing to illustrate biblical truths; thus, they are never used apart from some teaching of Scripture. I will allow Edwards to speak for himself at some length, with only a few comments along the way, before drawing some conclusions about his use of a creational-theology approach to general revelation. Then in part 4, following Edwards's own guidance, I will indicate some ways that we might develop the disciplines of creational theology and improve our ability to "make haste so to live."

Examples from Edwards

Edwards believed that "there are many truths concerning God, and our duty to him, which are evident by the light of nature."[2] In his ministry of preaching and writing, Edwards took this belief to heart and made great use of the revelation of God in creation, in aspects of culture, and in the actions of men's consciences, in order to appeal to the hearts and minds of his hearers. In this section I want to briefly examine just a few examples from Edwards's works that illustrate his creational-theology approach to general revelation.

Trees Again

There is, for example, his use of a tree to illustrate the natural propensity of the creation to glorify God:

> Thus it appears reasonable to suppose, that it was God's last end, that there might be a glorious and abundant emanation of his infinite fulness of good *ad extra*, or without himself; and that the disposition to communicate himself, or diffuse his own FULNESS, was what moved him to create the world. But here I observe, that there would be some impropriety in saying, that a disposition in God to communicate himself *to the creature*, moved him to create the world. For an inclination in God to communicate himself to an *object*, seems to presuppose the *existence* of the object, at least in idea. But the diffusive disposition that excited God to give creatures existence, was rather a communicative *disposition* in general, or a disposition in the fulness of the divinity to flow out and diffuse itself. Thus the disposition there is in the root and stock of a tree to diffuse sap and life, is doubtless the reason of their communication to its buds, leaves, and fruits *after* these exist. But a disposition to communicate of its life and sap to its *fruits*, is not so properly the cause of its *producing* those fruits, as its disposition to diffuse its sap and life in general. Therefore, to speak strictly according to truth, we may suppose, *that a disposition in God, as an original property of his nature, to an emanation of his own infinite fulness, was what excited him to create the world; and so, that the emanation itself was aimed at by him as a last end of the creation.*[3]

Here Edwards is guarding God from any appearance of *needing* anything that He has made. He does not need creatures to acknowledge His glory; He is sufficient unto Himself for His own glory. Rather, the fact that the creation reveals the glory of God is simply

141

an outgrowth of the divine propensity to diffuse His glory into all places, much as a tree sends its sap to leaves, buds, and fruit, not because it needs to do so, but simply because this is its natural disposition. As a tree does not create fruit in order to send sap to it, but rather sends sap to its fullest extremities, including its fruit, so God did not create the world to increase His glory. Rather, because He created the world, it is only natural that His glory would be expressed in and through it all.

Precious Gems

In this same book, Edwards turns to the example of a precious gem—an object of culture as opposed to creation—to illustrate the way in which God imparts His communicable attributes to people:

> Another emanation of divine fulness, is the communication of virtue and *holiness* to the creature: this is a communication of God's holiness; so that hereby the creature partakes of God's own moral excellency; which is properly the beauty of the divine nature. And as God delights in his own beauty, he must necessarily delight in the creature's holiness; which is a conformity to and participation of it, as truly as a brightness of a jewel, held in the sun's beams, is a participation or derivation of the sun's brightness, though immensely less in degree.[4]

The diamond has no inherent brightness; it cannot shine and be brilliant by itself. It requires the light of the sun to show off its various facets and reveal its beauty. But then, to a very large extent, the beauty of the diamond is really the glory of the sun's light, working in and through the diamond to show its own splendor. Just so the virtue and holiness that we discover in the lives of people around us are expressions of God's glory, being attributes communicated from Him to them, and manifested *through* them by His Spirit at work *in* them. God delights to see Himself thus reflected in His creatures, and we should be quick to glorify and praise Him whenever such attributes come to light. We must not think that such divine radiance in any way originates with us; people are, rather, the reflection of the light and glory of God, to whom alone praise is due.

Illustrations from the Animals

In a tightly reasoned illustration from the realm of the animal kingdom in his sermon on Psalm 94:8–11, Edwards pressed the point of man's fallenness, showing that something has occurred in the race of men to jar them from their original purpose:

> By this we may see how manifest are the *ruins* of the *fall* of man . . . The brute creatures, birds, beasts, fishes, and insects, though there be innumerable kinds of them, yet all seem to have such a degree of perception and perfection given them, as best suits their place in the creation, their manner of living and the ends for which they were made. There is no defect visible in them; they are perfect in their kind; there seems to be nothing wanting, in order to their filling up their allotted place in the world. And there can be no reasonable doubt but that it was so at first with mankind. It is not reasonable to suppose, that God would make many thousands of kinds of creatures in this lower world, and one kind the highest of them all, to be the head of the rest; and that all the rest should be complete in their kinds, every way endowed with such qualifications as are proportioned to their use and end: and only this most noble creature of all, left exceeding imperfect, notoriously destitute of what he principally stands in need of to answer the end of his being. The principal faculty by which God has distinguished this noble creature from the rest, is his understanding: but would God so distinguish man in his creation from other creatures, and then seal up that understanding with such an extreme blindness, as to render it useless, as to the principal ends of it; and wholly to disenable him from answering the ends of an intelligent creature, and to make his understanding rather a misery than a blessing to him; and rendering him much more mischievous than useful? Therefore, if the Scripture had not told us so, yet we might safely conclude, that mankind are not now, as they were made at first; but that they are in a *fallen* state or condition.[5]

Why does man alone, of all the creatures of God, not function properly according to his special gift and calling? Why does his use of reason lead him to error and mischief, rather than to the knowledge of God and His glory, when all the other creatures perform their appointed roles so ably? It can only be that man is not now living as he was created to live, as God intended. He has fallen from his original state into a marred and miserable existence, from which not even his greatest and unique gift can extricate him.

Appeal to a Dam

In his well-known sermon "Sinners in the Hands of an Angry God," in which occurs the famous illustration of a spider dangled over fire, Edwards sought to impress on his hearers the danger in which they stood of God's wrath breaking out against them at any moment. He appealed to another artifact of culture, a man-made dam, to make his point:

> The wrath of God is like great waters that are dammed for the present; they increase more and more, and rise higher and higher, till an outlet is given; and the longer the stream is stopped, the more rapid and mighty is its course, when once it is let loose. It is true, that judgment against your evil works has not been executed hitherto; the floods of God's vengeance have been withheld; but your guilt in the mean time is constantly increasing, and you are every day treasuring up more wrath; the waters are constantly rising, and waxing more and more mighty; and there is nothing but the mere pleasure of God, that holds the waters back, that are unwilling to be stopped, and press hard to go forward. If God should only withdraw his hand from the flood-gate, it would immediately fly open, and the fiery floods of the fierceness and wrath of God would rush forth with inconceivable fury, and would come upon you with omnipotent power; and if your strength were ten thousand times greater than it is, yea, ten thousand times greater than the strength of the stoutest, sturdiest devil in hell, it would be nothing to withstand or endure it.[6]

Illustration of Fire

A rather more extensive and ingenious illustration of God's wrath occurs in Edwards's sermon on Isaiah 33:14. Here Edwards employs cross-cultural and highly personal uses of fire to strike fear in the souls of his hearers concerning the enormity of God's wrath against their sins. He appeals both to an artifact of culture—fire—and to the actions of men's consciences in response to it:

The fire into which men are to be cast is called a *furnace of fire*. Furnaces are contrived for an extreme degree of heat, this being necessary for the purposes for which they are designed, as the running and refining of metals, and the melting of materials into glass. The fire of such earthly furnaces may be called *devouring fire*, as the heat of some of them is such, that in them even stones will presently be dissolved. Now, if a person should be brought to the mouth of such a furnace, and there should see how the fire glows, so as presently to make every thing cast into it all over white and bright with fire, and at the same time should know that he was immediately to be cast into this furnace, would not fearfulness surprise him?

In some heathen countries, the manner of disposing of dead bodies is to dig a great pit, to put in it a great quantity of fuel, to put the dead bodies on the pile, and to set it on fire. This is some image of the burning of dead souls in the pit of hell. Now, if a person were brought to the edge of such a pit, filled with glowing flames, to be immediately cast into it, would it not surprise the heart with fearfulness?

The flames of a very great fire, as when a house is all on fire, give one some idea of the fierceness of the wrath of God: such is the rage of flames. And we see that the greater a fire is, the fiercer is its heat in every part; and the reason is, because one part heats another. The heat in a particular place, besides the heat which proceeds out of the fuel in that place, is increased by the additional heat of the fire all around it. Hence we may conceive something of what fierceness the fire will be, when this visible world shall be turned into one great furnace. That will be devouring fire indeed . . .

Men can artificially raise such a degree of heat with burning glasses, as will quickly melt the very stones and sand. And it is probable that the heat of that great fire which will burn the world, will be such as to melt the rocks, and the very ground, and turn them into a kind of liquid fire: so that the whole world will probably be converted into a great lake, or liquid globe of fire, a vast ocean of fire, in which the wicked shall be overwhelmed. It will be an ocean of fire, which will always be in a tempest, in which the wicked shall be tossed to and fro, having no

145

rest day nor night, vast waves or billows of fire continually rolling over their heads.

But this will be only an *image* of that dreadful fire of the wrath of God, which the wicked shall at the same time suffer in their *souls*.[7]

The implication is clear: If we draw back at the prospect of being exposed to such intense heat in our flesh, how much more ought we to fear the prospect of our very souls' being subjected to such fiery wrath from God?

The Example of God with Job

In an interesting passage in his sermon on Psalm 46:10, Edwards points out how God Himself appealed to the creation to rebuke Job for his insolence and lack of faith and to call him back to a proper sub- mission to and trust in divine grace and providence. God did not expound any special revelation to convince his servant, as we have seen, but only took him on a grand tour of the creation, pointing out creature after creature, and His own role in their creation and suste- nance, to recall Job to faith.[8]

Clocks, Wheels, and the Planets

Edwards's book *An Humble Attempt* includes a brilliant illustra- tion that compares the history of nations to the workings of a clock, a wheel, and the motions of heavenly bodies to demonstrate how all of history is moving toward a great denouement:

All the changes brought to pass in the world, from age to age, are ordered by infinite wisdom, in one respect or other to prepare the way for that glorious issue of things, when truth and righteousness shall finally pre- vail, and he, whose right it is, shall take the kingdom. All the creatures, in all their operations and motions, continually tend to this. As in a clock, all the motions of the whole system of wheels and movements, tend to the striking of the hammer at the appointed time. All the revo- lutions and restless motions of the sun and other heavenly bodies, from day to day, from year to year, and from age to age, are continually tend- ing thither; as all the many turnings of a chariot, in a journey, tend to the appointed journey's end. The mighty struggles and conflicts of nations, those vast successive changes which are brought to pass in the kingdoms and empires of the world, from one age to another, as it were, travail-pangs of the creation, in order to bring forth this glorious event. And the Scriptures represent the last struggles and changes that shall immediately precede this event, as being the greatest of all; as the last pangs of a woman in travail are the most violent.[9]

The Rainbow

Two more examples will suffice to illustrate Edwards's wide use of general revelation in his preaching and writing. The first, from his *Notes on the Bible*, is an extensive explanation of the fitness of the rainbow in Genesis 9 as an illustration of God's grace. Here Edwards gets very close to the limits of the grammatico-historico-cultural method of interpretation, and seems almost to veer off into the realm of allegory. Yet all along the way he supports his conclusions with additional references to Scripture, thus making it very difficult to charge him with any violation of sound exegetical practice.

He says that the rainbow is a perfect token of God's covenant of grace because it captures and diffuses the light that symbolizes God's favor and leads His people to hope, joy, and praise. The different colors of light in a rainbow represent "the sweetness of the divine Spirit of love, and those amiable sweet graces and happy influences that are from that Spirit." The rainbow appears in a cloud, which symbolizes the divine presence, so as to shield us from brilliance too glorious to bear—like Christ, the exact representation of God, appearing in the form of a man. The light of a rainbow is pleasant and comes after a storm, as clouds are dissolving, having disgorged their blessings on the earth, as Christ did while he was dying for our sins. The cloud also represents for Edwards the church, composed as it is of innumerable drops of vapor, which reflect the light of the sun in many and diverse ways. The beauty of a rainbow reminds us that the wrath of God has been turned away from His people. If completed, a rainbow would be a perfect circle, like the church in her fullness, with God, the sun, at the center, as in Revelation 4. And so on.[10]

Appeal to Light Itself

Finally, in a sermon on John 5:35, Edwards appeals to light itself to explain the unique purpose and calling of a minister of the gospel. Christ is the light of the world, and just as there is one great light in the solar system that illumines and sustains all else, so Christ is the light of His church. Ministers of the gospel are like stars (cf. Rev. 1:20), reflecting the light of Christ into the darkness of the world. He is the great flame from which the lamps of those who hold out the light of the gospel take their oil. By casting the light they receive from Christ, ministers make things manifest in the souls of men; they refresh and delight those dwelling in darkness; and they give direction to those seeking their way.[11]

Now, the fact that all these examples are little more than sermon illustrations need not detract from their appropriateness for instructing us about the proper use of general revelation within a creational-theology mode. Edwards intended them to carry a great deal of weight in the communication of divine truth, as is shown in the breadth of these examples, drawing as they do from creation, culture, and the actions of human conscience; the care, and the depth to which they are developed; their familiarity with the hearers; and the thoughtful and highly reasoned way in which Edwards employs them. It is readily apparent that Edwards had a high regard for the revelation of God coming at him from the creation in all its aspects. It should be equally apparent that, in pressing this revelation upon his hearers, Edwards believed it could accomplish purposes in harmony with the ministry of the Word and the proclamation of the gospel. What were those purposes, and how did Edwards justify them?

Edwards on the Uses of Creational Theology

We can discern in Edwards's practice two purposes or uses of this creational-theology approach to general revelation: awakening God's elect and strengthening His redeemed. In each of these uses, the creational theology of Edwards enables him to improve the doctrine of general revelation and recover the purposes for which God gives it.

Awakening the Elect

Edwards was continually mindful of the fact that members of his congregation were yet unregenerate. He understood that not even all those who professed faith in Christ could be safely counted among the redeemed of the Lord. As he said in introducing the application section of his sermon "Sinners in the Hands of an Angry God," "The use of this awful subject may be for awakening unconverted persons in this congregation."[12] In his sermon on Romans 5:10 he described his hearers as "enemies of God" who have taken His grace for granted and are "poor, unworthy, unlovely" creatures.[13] He believed that these appeals to general revelation, in the context of the preaching of the Word and the proclamation of the gospel, could serve the purposes of spiritual awakening in those unregenerate ones who may have been among the elect of God.

In particular he seems to have wanted to increase in them the fear of the Lord and thus to drive them to seek mercy and grace from Him, which, as he repeatedly assured them, God was all too ready to give. Here are the opening comments of his appeal in a sermon on Acts 16:29–30:

> There is nothing which you see, but what may justly minister torment to you, while you remain in a natural condition. If you lift up your eyes, and behold the sun, moon, and stars, and cast your eyes abroad on the face of the earth, and see the mountains, and fields, and trees, it may justly put you in mind of the dolefulness of your condition; that the great God, who made all these things, who stretched forth the heavens as a curtain, who ordained the sun, moon, and stars, and laid the foundations of the earth, and causes the grass and trees to grow; is a God in whom you have no interest, but who is continually angry with you, and that his wrath abides on you. So when you look on your own body, and consider how it is formed and contrived, it may be a frightful thing to you to consider, that he who made you is not at peace with you, and that you are the object of his displeasure. If you have pleasures and enjoyments, and are in flourishing circumstances, if you see the faces of your near friends and dear relations, and look upon your children and other dear friends, and behold your costly possessions, these things may justly minister torment to you, while you are in a natural state. For

149

consider, that you do not know but that all these things are given you in wrath. When you sit down to eat and drink, you may do it in torment, because you know not but that this may be in wrath. When you lie down upon your beds, it may justly be in torment, for you do not know but you shall awake in hell. And when you awake in the morning, it may justly be with torment in your heart, to think you are still in that doleful condition. When you go forth to your daily labour, you have reason to go with a terrified heart; for you know not but you are followed with God's curse in all that to which you put your hands. Whatever dispensations of Providence you may have, all may justly put you in mind of the dolefulness of your condition.[14]

Given Edwards's Reformed perspective on general revelation—that unregenerate men refuse to acknowledge the revelation of God in creation—how could he justify such incessant, detailed, and urgent appeals to creation, culture, and the ways of conscience as tools for pressing the truth of Scripture on the hearts and minds of his hearers? Is he not in danger of falling into the error of the maximizers of general revelation, looking to the revelation of God in creation to establish a knowledge of God, and from there to acceptance of the gospel? If not, how does he avoid this?

Again, through the doctrine of election: because he believed that God had chosen to save certain people from before the foundation of the world, Edwards knew that God would actually do so in His own way and time. His responsibility, as one of Christ's "stars," was to reflect as much light, from as many sources as possible, on the pathways of the unregenerate elect, so that the Spirit of God would have much to work with in effectually calling them to saving faith.

The Wooing of God's Spirit

Edwards understood from Scripture that God's Spirit was at work among the unregenerate, striving with them and wooing certain ones of them to the true knowledge of God. In a sermon on Romans 3:19 he went to great lengths to show his hearers the many ways in which God was actually striving with them:

God has tried you with a great deal of kindness, and he never has sincerely been thanked by you for any of it. God has watched over you, and preserved you, and provided for you, and followed you with mercy all your days; and yet you have continued sinning against him. He has given you food and raiment, but you have improved both for the service of sin. He has preserved you while you slept; but when you arose, it was to return to the old trade of sinning. God, notwithstanding this ingratitude, has still continued his mercy; but his kindness has never won your heart, or brought you to a more grateful behaviour towards him. It may be you have received many remarkable mercies, recoveries from sickness, or preservations of your life when exposed by accidents, when if you had died, you would have gone directly to hell; but you never had any true thankfulness for any of those mercies. God has kept you out of hell, and continued your day of grace, and offers of salvation, so long a time; while you did not regard your own salvation so much as in secret to ask God for it. And now God has greatly added to his mercy to you, by giving you the strivings of his Spirit, whereby a most precious opportunity for your salvation is in your hands. But what thanks has God received for it?[15]

This wooing of God, Edwards insisted, has been both from the preaching of the Word *and* from the revelation of God in creation: "God has called earnestly and for a long time; he has called and called again in his word, and in his providence, and you have refused."[16]

Edwards was convinced that this striving and wooing of the Spirit was the ordinary way that God brought men to Himself, and that it included appeals from both books of revelation:

This is God's ordinary way before great and signal expressions of his mercy and favour. He very commonly so orders it in his providence, and so influences men by his Spirit, that they are brought to see their miserable condition as they are in themselves, and to despair of help from themselves, or from an arm of flesh, before he appears for them, and also makes them sensible of their sin, and their unworthiness of God's help.[17]

151

But, we might ask, how does this striving and wooing work, given our understanding of general revelation and sinful men? Edwards answers a little later on in this same sermon:

> It may be inquired, How God assists natural conscience so as to convince the sinner of his desert of hell? I answer,
>
> In general, it is by light. The whole work of God is carried on in the heart of man from his first convictions to his conversion by light. It is by discoveries which are made to his soul. But by what light is it, that a sinner is made sensible that he deserves God's wrath? It is some discovery that he has, which makes him sensible of the heinousness of disobeying and casting contempt upon God. The light which gives evangelical humiliation, and which makes man sensible of the hateful and odious nature of sin, is a discovery of God's glory and excellence and grace. But what is it which a natural man sees of God, which makes him sensible that sin against God deserves his wrath; for he sees nothing of the excellence and loveliness of God's glory and grace? I answer,
>
> Particularly, it seems to be discovery of God's awful and terrible greatness. Natural men cannot see any thing of God's loveliness, his amiable and glorious grace, or any thing which should attract their love; but they may see his terrible greatness to excite their terror. Wicked men in another world, though they do not see his loveliness and grace, yet they see his awful greatness, and that makes them sensible of the heinousness of sin.[18]

Edwards appears to be banking on the apostle Paul's insistence that all men do have a knowledge of God—of His deity and power—and that even though they suppress that knowledge, they never quite manage to get away from it. Edwards, in his many appeals to general revelation, summons that knowledge from the shadowy depths of the unregenerate soul to insist again and again that what the soul knows by virtue of its being in the image of God is true—and terrible! While the sinful heart strives mightily to suppress the knowledge of God, even among the unregenerate elect, God's Spirit strives all the more mightily to break down their defenses and draw His chosen ones to Himself. They continue, like the apostle Paul, kicking against the goads of God; yet His power will inevitably prevail, and the accumulating brilliance of the light of revelation—in creation, Scripture, and the gospel—will, in God's time, overwhelm all resistance in the hearts of His elect, overpower their rebellious spirits, break through to their understandings, and capture their hearts. The numerous seasons of spiritual harvest that Edwards experienced during his years in Northampton would seem to vindicate his use of general revelation in a creational-theology mode. In appealing to the unregenerate elect, Edwards drew heavily on familiar aspects of creation, culture, and the human conscience as means whereby the Spirit of God, in the context of the exposition of Scripture and the proclamation of the gospel, might finally prevail to gather His chosen ones to Himself.

Edwards's use of general revelation thus avoids the pitfalls of certain maximizers of this doctrine by not depending on it alone as a way of establishing a degree of consent as to the existence of God, as a kind of first step toward the proclamation of the gospel. Rather, Edwards, with the exposition of Scripture as the framework and the proclamation of the gospel of Jesus Christ as the constant touchstone and battering ram of the recalcitrant heart, appealed to general revelation from the perspective of one who sees creation for what it is, and calls upon his hearers—rebellious image-bearers of God in denial of what they know to be true—to see it that way as well.

For the Benefit of the Redeemed

But Edwards believed that a creational-theology approach to general revelation could benefit the redeemed of the Lord too. Here he shows those who have tended to minimize this doctrine how its proper use can further the work of the gospel among the redeemed. We will observe three uses of this doctrine in strengthening those who have already come to a saving knowledge of the Lord and are thus readily able to see the revelation of God in creation, culture, and the ways of men for what it is.

First, Edwards marked out certain spiritual benefits that might accrue to the souls of those who are increasing in familiarity with and understanding of the general revelation of God.

A *help in times of temptation.* Edwards himself found a refuge in general revelation from attacks of temptation and sinful thoughts. He resolved, "When I am violently beset with temptation, or cannot rid myself of evil thoughts, to do something in arithmetic, or geometry, or some other study, which necessarily engages all my thoughts, and unavoidably keeps them from wandering."[19] It is perhaps not too difficult to see how such a study could be helpful, especially when one enters into the study with the understanding that what he is contemplating—problems in math, the beauty of geometry, the wonders of science, and so forth—conveys true information about the faithfulness, power, beauty, majesty, and wonder of God.

A *stimulus to improved thought.* Related to this, Edwards found such studies to be helpful in improving his thinking in general. By going out among the glory of God in the creation, he discovered that his mind was stimulated and exercised in such a way as to improve it for other uses: "I find by conversing on natural philosophy, that I gain knowledge abundantly faster, and see the reasons of things much more clearly, than in private study . . ."[20] Note also his comment that this exercising of his mind is most effectively achieved in conversation with others, a point to which we will return in chapter 7.

Improved appreciation of beauty. Similarly, Edwards found that his investigations of general revelation enhanced his ability to appreciate true beauty:

> That which is beautiful, considered by itself separately, and deformed, considered as a part of something else more extended; or beautiful, only with respect to itself and a few other things, and not as a part of that which contains all things—the Universe;—is false beauty and a confined beauty. That which is beautiful, with respect to the university of things, has a generally extended excellence and true beauty; that the more extended, or limited, its system is, the more confined or extended is its beauty.[21]

True beauty, in other words, can be determined only against the wide backdrop of the creation as God has given it. Something cannot be considered truly beautiful if it merely has reference to a small universe

154

of things. True beauty is discerned by observing beauty far and wide in the creation, and then comparing what we are observing with the patterns of beauty in creation. Edwards cannot possibly have been thinking of postmodern art in this observation, yet his comments could not be more salient with respect to it. Beauty is not merely in the eye of the beholder, as many contemporary artists want to insist; true beauty is discovered in patterns of conformity to and imitation of the beauty with which God has infused His great creation. If we ignore that beauty, or are unable to discern it, we will have difficulty appreciating any beauty whatsoever.

Sources of general revelation. As we have seen, in his own use of general revelation, Edwards resorted to natural science, to reading, studying, and thinking about problems of mathematics, geometry, and natural philosophy. He also found insight and encouragement in the study of church history:

> My heart has been much on the advancement of Christ's kingdom in the world. The histories of the past advancement of Christ's kingdom have been sweet to me. When I have read histories of past ages, the pleasantest thing, in all my reading, has been, to read of the kingdom of Christ being promoted. And when I have expected, in my reading, to come to any such thing, I have rejoiced in the prospect, all the way as I read. And my mind has been much entertained and delighted with the scripture promises and prophecies, which relate to the future glorious advancement of Christ's kingdom upon earth.[22]

Above all, however, Edwards seems to have benefited from being out among the things of creation, in the forests, among the trees, and with the animals. The following account of one such experience should encourage us all as to the ability of God's revelation in creation to minister powerfully to the souls of His redeemed:

> Once, as I rode out into the woods for my health, in 1737, having alighted from my horse in a retired place, as my manner commonly has been, to walk for divine contemplation and prayer, I had a view, that for me was extraordinary, of the glory of the Son of God, as Mediator between God and man, and his wonderful, great, full, pure and sweet

155

grace and love, and meek and gentle condescension. This grace that appeared so calm and sweet, appeared also great above the heavens. The person of Christ appeared ineffably excellent, with an excellency great enough to swallow up all thought and conception—which continued, as near as I can judge, about an hour; which kept me the greater part of the time in a flood of tears, and weeping aloud. I felt an ardency of soul to be, what I know not otherwise how to express, emptied and annihilated; to lie in the dust, and to be full of Christ alone; to love him with a holy and pure love; to trust in him; to live upon him, to serve and follow him; and to be perfectly sanctified and made pure, with a divine and heavenly purity. I have several other times had views very much of the same nature, which have had the same effects.[23]

Who among the redeemed of the Lord would not wish for such experiences of the love of Christ to nurture and strengthen their weary souls? It was not in the study, not in conversation with others, not even in public worship that Edwards experienced such an overwhelming presence of God and assurance of His grace, but amid the beauties of creation, as he walked, prayed, and meditated on God's Word.

Second, besides providing encouragement to and strengthening of the soul, Edwards believed that immersion in the revelation of God in creation, culture, and the ways of men could lead to greater knowledge of God and conformity to His image. As we saw previously, he wrote of the revelation of God in creation:

There are many reasons to think that what God has in view, in an increasing communication of himself through eternity, is an *increasing* knowledge of God, love to him, and joy in him. And it is to be considered, that the more those divine communications *increase* in the creature, the more it becomes one with God: for so much the more is it united to God in love, the heart is drawn nearer and nearer to God, and the union with him becomes more firm and close: and, at the same time, the creature becomes more and more *conformed* to God.[24]

The revelation of God in general revelation can communicate true knowledge of God. The more of that revelation we receive and understand according to how God intends it—an ability unique to the redeemed—the more we can expect to increase in love for God and union with Him, and the more we will be conformed to His image. Not only will our souls be encouraged, but we will actually experience progress in sanctification, as the general revelation of God in creation, culture, and the ways of men enables us to see more clearly and embrace more wholeheartedly what God is revealing about Himself in His Word and in the gospel.

Finally, Edwards made use of general revelation within a mode of creational theology to nurture gratitude among his parishioners and, perhaps, to stimulate them to greater compassion for the lost. In the application section of his sermon on Acts 16:29–30, immediately following his fervent appeal to the lost to consider the greatness of God toward them in His works of providence, Edwards counseled the redeemed—"the truly penitent"—to consider how such contemplations might elevate their souls to thanks and praise, and lead them to a more compassionate consideration of the plight of the lost:

> This subject may well excite joy and thankfulness in the hearts of the truly penitent, that God has found a way to deliver them from such a condition; that God has been pleased to send his Son into the world to die for them; that he has given them the gospel and the means of grace; and that he has delivered them from this dreadful condition.[25]

Surely this is a benefit not to be taken lightly by those in whom the grace of God has worked to lead them to lives of gratitude and mission in the Lord.

Thus Edwards issues a rebuke to the minimizers of general revelation that there is much benefit to be gained by those who have come to a saving knowledge of Christ in becoming increasingly familiar with the revelation of God in creation, culture, and the ways of men. As Hopkins reminded us, even in the sunlight that greets and warms us each day there is glory to be observed and praise to be rendered to God. Surely, indeed, "this is a thing to live for." That being so, let us then "make haste so to live." It remains for us to consider how, following

157

Edwards's practice and counsel, we might begin to take up the happy task of creational theology, of pursuing the knowledge of God as He is revealing it in creation, culture, and the actions of men's consciences.

Questions for Study or Discussion

1. How would you assess the examples of Edwards's use of general revelation provided in this chapter? Do you think they were effective? Why or why not?

2. Do you think it is possible for others to make such observations? How might learning to do so benefit them? How might taking up this discipline serve to nurture your own faith?

3. How does Edwards's use of general revelation in a creational theology mode issue a corrective to the maximizers of general revelation? How does it serve to rebuke the minimizers? Where would you put yourself between those two poles? How does Edwards's example minister to you?

4. Edwards primarily used examples of general revelation that would be familiar to his hearers—ordinary, simple, everyday things. What would have been the advantage of his doing this? Would doing this have had benefit beyond the time that they were actually listening to him preach?

5. Look back at the goals you set for yourself in this study. Are you making any progress? Do you feel as though you are learning anything that might help you in your own walk with the Lord? Explain.

The Happy Task of Creational Theology

Activity 6

Some of the best "creational theologians" of the Christian tradition are the hymn-writers. The great hymns of the Christian tradition sparkle with references to creation, culture, and the actions of conscience in helping us to know and praise the Lord. Spend an hour or so with a hymnal. In your notebook, record several hymns' references to general revelation, and offer some comments concerning the hymn-writers' creational-theology approach to general revelation. What are they trying to do for us as we sing these hymns? How do the lyrics help us to enter more fully into the knowledge of God? Sing one or two of the hymns you selected, keeping in mind the writer's purpose in this particular application of creational theology. How is your appreciation for each hymn enhanced? Your love for God and praise to Him? Meet with your conversation partner to share your experience and conclusions.

THE HAPPY TASK OF CREATIONAL THEOLOGY

Logos

The utter regularity of it all!
How summer in its turn gives way to fall,

the fall to winter, spring, and summer; then
the unfailing cycle starts its course again,

the night succumbing to the day, the day
to night. So life to death at last gives way,

albeit suddenly and brutally
at times. As when today, a sparrow's free,

unfettered flight was interrupted by
my plate glass door, and he was left to die

in stunned, astonished gasps upon my deck.
I warmed him in my hands, his broken neck

beyond repair, and held him as the light
departed from his eyes, and death's cold night

descended. Light to darkness, warmth to cold,
unfailing regularity as old

as being itself. And every sparrow's fall
somehow fulfills a purpose in it all.

7

PRACTICING CREATIONAL THEOLOGY (1): ADVICE FROM JONATHAN EDWARDS

"Consider the lilies . . ."
—Matthew 6:28

That which the Creator intended should be our main employment, is something above what he intended the beast for, and therefore hath given us superior powers. Therefore, without doubt, it should be a considerable part of our business to improve those superior faculties. But the faculty by which we are chiefly distinguished from the brutes, is the faculty of understanding. It follows then, that we should make it our chief business to improve this faculty, and should by no means prosecute it as a business by the bye.

—Jonathan Edwards[1]

One spirit—His
Who wore the platted thorns with bleeding brows—
Rules universal nature. Not a flower

But shows some touch, in freckle, streak, or stain,
Of his unrivall'd pencil. He inspires
Their balmy odors, and imparts their hues,
And bathes their eyes with nectar, and includes
In grains as countless as the seaside sands,
The forms with which he sprinkles all the earth.
Happy who walks with him! whom what he finds
Of flavor or of scent in fruit or flower,
Of what he views of beautiful or grand
In nature, from the broad majestic oak
To the green blade that twinkles in the sun,
Prompts with remembrance of a present God.
His presence, who made all so fair, perceived,
Makes all fairer still.

—The Task, 6.238–54

A Stewardship Forfeited

That evangelical Christians have abandoned large sectors of the field of serious and creative thinking to the barbarians of the modernist and postmodernist intellectual community is no longer news. The world as we see it, as we encounter and have to deal with it day by day— from the things we own to the work we do to the environment in which we live and the human cultures and struggles that exist in it—is today largely defined and held captive by a mind-set of naturalism and relativism, the emblems of our emerging postmodern condition. While some evangelical and Reformed thinkers and scholars have attempted raids on various redoubts of the entrenched secular and postmodern positions, for the most part these remain captive under banners hostile to the God of Scripture. Meanwhile, the forces of the army of the Lord have been largely content to relinquish the field of intellectual struggle to the howling hordes of humanistic hubris. We have retreated into a kind of narrow pietism to warm our hands around dim fires of faith and to seek comfort for our souls. Mark Noll observes:

164

Despite dynamic success at a popular level, modern American evangelicals have failed notably in sustaining serious intellectual life. They have nourished millions of believers in the simple verities of the gospel but have largely abandoned the universities, the arts, and other realms of "high" culture. Even in its more progressive and culturally upscale subgroups, evangelicalism has little intellectual muscle.[2]

What is true among the intellectual leadership of the evangelical world is true as well among the members of the body of Christ in general: We have relinquished the task of naming the creatures and ordering the affairs of God's world to those who, by virtue of their unregenerate blindness, have no ability to see the creation for what it is and to order it according to its divine purposes and ends. We have forfeited our stewardship as the caretakers and guardians of God's creation.

Theology in a State of Languor

Theology in general (which, as we have seen, is an inescapable task and calling for the followers of Christ) and creational theology in particular are today in a state of languor among those for whom these disciplines are intended by God—His people. There is little zeal among lay men and women for the serious work of theological study. Their schedules are too crowded with other matters—most of which have little, if any, eternal significance—and what study of God's Word they do engage in is narrowly focused on helping to enhance their sense of personal well-being in the world. If they read, it is the pop theology of writers who labor to put some new and more interesting spin on the life of faith, and whose books are snapped up and read by the millions, yet without much discernible effect on the body of Christ or its calling and mission. The marginalization of the church continues in spite of the brisk sales of Christian literature year in and year out.

The Hope of Creational Theology

This is a situation from which a healthy creational theology can help to deliver us. In the preceding chapters I have sought to present the biblical necessity and promise of this exciting field of endeavor. God

165

commands us to take up the task of knowing Him through the things He has made, so that we might worship Him more completely and serve Him more faithfully. This is the calling of everyone who knows the Lord through faith in Jesus Christ. And while it is a difficult and demanding task, yet it is one that can fill our lives with greater hope, joy, and delight than any of the many distractions and diversions that now keep us from fulfilling our calling in this area.

We cannot fail to see, for example, in Jonathan Edwards's approach to general revelation—his practice of creational theology—a deep sense of delight and confidence. As he appeals broadly and powerfully to aspects of creation, culture, and conscience to help illuminate the teaching of God's Word for the people in his charge, we sense his own hope and joy brimming. Edwards truly reveled in seeing God in the works of His hand. He sought out as much of the knowledge of God in general revelation as time and resources would permit. And he brought the observations and conclusions of his renewed mind to the constant attention of his hearers, thus leading them to consider the line of God going out in the things He has made, and inviting them to join him in his revelry before the providential throne. It is no mere accident that God honored Edwards and his congregation with two powerful seasons of revival during the time of his ministry there. Edwards's example holds out hope that we also might rediscover something of the joys of knowing God through the revelation that He is making of Himself in creation, culture, and the ways of conscience. He encourages us to think, as he and Cowper did, that we can learn to rejoice and give thanks for everything around us that "prompts with remembrance of a present God."

But is there anything more than what can be gained by his example that we might learn of this matter from Edwards? Can he offer us any specific advice about how we might begin to take up the happy task of creational theology and "make haste" to begin discovering the glory of God in everything we experience each day?

Edwards on Christian Knowledge

In his sermon "Christian Knowledge," Edwards argues a powerful case for the careful and serious study of divinity as the most important intellectual task to which a believer can devote himself. The reading and study of Scripture and sacred theology are far more important than most believers consider, and should be undertaken with greater earnestness and consistency by all the members of the body of Christ. In this sermon Edwards observes that there is much to be learned from God's general revelation, but that without the perspective of divinity, none of this is intelligible. In "Christian Knowledge," Edwards offers us no direct guidance on how to improve our ability to discern the line of God going out in the things he has made. His focus is entirely on improving our knowledge of Scripture and sacred theology.

Yet in the advice he gives at the end of his sermon concerning how to proceed in this most important endeavor, we can discern an outline for thinking about how to begin taking up the happy task of creational theology. In this chapter, the first of three on the practice of creational theology, I want to consider Edwards's seven recommendations for growing in the knowledge of divinity and suggest some ways that we, following his own example, might apply these guidelines to the work of creational theology. Then in chapter 8, we will discuss the practice of creational theology and make some suggestions about how to pursue this discipline consistently in the light of our relationship with and calling from the Lord Jesus Christ. Finally, in chapter 9, we will bring our study of creational theology to a conclusion, by examining the role of this happy task with respect to our overarching calling to glorify God in all things.

A Question of Time

Before proceeding to Edwards's sermon on Christian knowledge, however, we should prepare for the necessity of having to make adjustments in the way we currently use the time that God has allotted us. Certainly we can imagine that we will have to make different use of our time than is perhaps presently the case with many of us. As Barry Morrow has observed,

> most Christians are caught up in the everydayness of life, a refusal to
> stop and reflect on significant issues, such as whether God exists and

167

what role He might play. Rather, they are trapped by the tyranny of the urgent and consequently are too busy to reflect on the transcendent.[3]

But as Edwards elsewhere notes,

you are accountable to God for your time. Time is a talent given us by God; he hath set us our day; and it is not for nothing, our day was appointed for some work; therefore he will, at the day's end, call us to an account. We must give account to him of the improvement of all our time.[4]

If we have resolved to "covenant with our eyes" to discover and delight in the revelation of God in creation, culture, and the acts of conscience, then we must be prepared to reclaim whatever time may be necessary for us to practice the disciplines that will enable us to carry out that commitment. Especially, Edwards counsels, should we make certain that our time is wisely invested in improving knowledge of God, and in the study of divinity and those Christian practices that are most conducive to it. Edwards would have us not squander the rest of our time in mere business or mindless diversions, as important or interesting as those may be. Ours is principally the business of the soul, Edwards observes, and all our time should be made subservient to the purposes of nurturing our souls in the knowledge of God, in order to "fit the mind and body for the work of our general and particular callings."[5]

So we must settle in our minds that some things in the way we use our time are going to have to change. Whatever those changes might be, if we can devote them to the disciplines necessary for carrying out our commitment to seek the Lord in His general revelation, they will be improvements in our time. And though our time may begin more and more to be taken up with hard work, yet it will yield the fruit of a deeper relationship with God and greater hope, joy, and power in our walk with Him.[6]

Open the Book

Edwards's first guideline for improving Christian knowledge is: "Be assiduous in reading the Holy Scriptures."[7] If we want to know what

God would say to us concerning Himself, His purposes, and His ways, we must turn to that Book in which He makes known to us as much of His will as He is pleased to reveal. We must open the Book of special revelation and "become well acquainted with the Scriptures" in all their parts if we would gain the knowledge of God that leads to Christian maturity. But we must open the book of general revelation as well.

Search the Scriptures Concerning General Revelation

This is excellent advice for beginning to study God's Word with respect to His general revelation in creation, culture, and conscience. Scripture has much to say about the subject of general revelation, as we have seen, and its teachings suggest guidelines for observing the line of God in the things He has made, and for reaching conclusions with respect to what we see. Many, many passages of the Word hold wisdom for thinking about His revelation in creation, culture, and the actions of conscience. A few that come to mind are Job 38 through 41, Psalms 29 and 104, Acts 14:14–17, and Acts 17:24–31. But these are just a few. As we study these and many other passages to learn how to think about general revelation, we can begin to identify principles, guidelines, and ways of thinking that will be helpful as we turn to general revelation itself. Above all, we will be reinforced in our conviction that only in the light of God's Word and the gospel can we make any sense whatsoever of what we are observing of Him in the things He has made. We will have more to say about this in our next chapter.

Open the Book of the World

As with all other knowledge of God, we must begin the happy task of creational theology in the study of God's Word and sacred theology. But Edwards's *practice* suggests that he felt much the same way about the revelation of God in the book of the world. While he did not spend as much time studying and thinking about such things as natural philosophy, church history, aesthetics, culture, and the creation, still, all his works make it plain that his mind had been much devoted to studying these areas and many others, and to thinking about

169

them in the light of Scripture and the gospel. Thus, we might expect him to counsel us to "open the book" of general revelation and begin to become familiar with all its parts if we would discover what God is saying to us there. What might that involve?

Look to your calling. To begin with, we might ask: Which aspects of God's general revelation most seem to have a bearing on His calling for me? Each of us has a calling from the Lord to serve Him in some vocation in life. And each of us has been sent into a personal mission field where we serve as agents of God's grace to the people we encounter each day. The demands and opportunities of that calling and field can be a good guide as to where to begin in opening the book of the world to see the glory of God being revealed there.

Ask yourself: As I think about my daily walk with the Lord, the work He has given me to do, the people before whom and the times within which I live, where might I turn to discern the line of God and learn to know and serve Him better through the things He has made? Which aspects of creation, culture, and the human conscience, if I could devote more time to studying and understanding them in the light of God's Word and the gospel, might yield deeper knowledge of the Creator? Which might better prepare me to fulfill my calling and to minister to the people in my personal mission field? I can't study everything, but I can do *something*. Which areas of study and further investigation will best help to equip me for my particular calling in the Lord?

From such questions the outline of a personal plan of study might begin to emerge that could help you make better use of your time in seeking the knowledge of God in general revelation. Paying more attention to the demands of work, the glories of your corner of God's creation, the interests of your peers, and the social and cultural issues of the day can be an excellent investment of your time for learning more about God and His purposes, truth, and ways.

Look to your interests. At the same time, certain subjects may appeal to you for one reason or another, even though they may have no practical utility in your calling and ministry. Perhaps you have always

170

wanted to know something about the arts and art history. Or you would like to know more about the flora and fauna of your particular area, or its natural or human history. Subjects of study that interest you can also be a part of your developing plan for taking back some of your time for the work of creational theology.

Seek out firsthand involvement. That plan could then lead you to firsthand involvement with the revelation of God in creation, culture, and the conscience. If your interest is in the creation around you, you might go out amid the plants, animals, and other features of your immediate environment, to learn about its creatures, experience them immediately, and ponder their unique contributions to the knowledge of God.[8] Your plan might lead you to take more interest in the people around you, encouraging you to spend more time getting to know them, listening to their stories, and discovering their particular interests and burdens. You might begin to pay more attention to the artifacts, institutions, and conventions of culture by which people today make their way in your community, and learn to meditate on what they may be showing you about God, His purposes, and His ways. Your plan might lead you to begin taking more interest in the issues and events of the day, seeking, like the sons of Issachar (1 Chron. 12:32), to understand our times with a view to discerning how God would have us act in them as His servants. Reading books and studying subjects is a good start. But being out in a forest, attending a symphony, or observing people in various kinds of settings will make those studies exceedingly more interesting and beneficial.

Becoming more "mindful." Improving our ability to discern the line of God in the things He has made must begin in study and direct experience of His revelation, both in the Book of Scripture and in the book of general revelation. And while this may require some adjusting of our time, more likely it will mean that we must begin simply to be more mindful of creation, culture, and the actions of conscience—perceiving, experiencing, and reflecting on them in the light of God's Word in order to discover in them what He may be revealing to us of

Himself, His purposes, and His ways. According to Harvard educator Ellen J. Langer, mindfulness involves three distinct activities.[9]

1. The first is the creation of new categories, which comes from paying closer attention to the people, contexts, and situations around us, looking for ways to organize our thoughts to help us make better sense of them. New categories will also enter our thinking as we take up the study of new subjects, or learn new skills of observation, conversation, and so forth.

2. The second activity is welcoming new information—meeting new people, observing new things, listening to new kinds of music, becoming interested in new ideas and issues. We must learn to receive the new information that comes from our firsthand reading of the book of the world with the same kind of enthusiasm that we have when we gain new insights from Scripture. Granted, seeing the glory of God in general revelation may take more time. Yet we expect it to be equally rewarding; therefore, we welcome our new knowledge with joy and treasure it deeply.

3. Finally, the mindful person is one who cultivates the ability to consider different perspectives, different points of view. Mindful people are good listeners. They try to understand what others are saying, not according to their own beliefs and views, but according to the people themselves. This makes it possible for them to enter into the thoughts and views of others more empathetically, and to learn from them and change their own views accordingly. Mindful people do not abandon their convictions; rather, they hold them in abeyance in order to understand others better and relate to them more effectively. One involved in creational theology with greater mindfulness will thus suspend judgment on such things as popular culture, the sometimes puzzling and contrary ways of people, and things with which they are unfamiliar until they can better understand these things according to their own divinely appointed purposes.

Believers taking up the happy task of creational theology would thus do well to cultivate greater mindfulness, together with better stewardship of their time, as they begin to open the book of general revelation and peruse its pages for what God may be revealing of Himself there.

Study and Compare

Edwards's second recommendation for improving Christian knowledge is as follows:

> Content not yourselves with only a cursory reading, without regarding the sense . . . When you read, observe what you read. Observe how things come in. Take note of the drift of the discourse, and compare one scripture with another.[10]

Again, we remind ourselves that Edwards is talking about the study of Scripture and sacred theology. His advice is sound: We should study nothing in isolation. God's revelation in Scripture is all of a piece; thus, we can gain the sense of it in any one place only by comparing what God has to say about the same subject in other places. As we thus compare Scripture with Scripture, we allow the Holy Spirit to bring increasing amounts of light to bear on the subject of our study, and we are more likely to gain the understanding that God wants us to have so that we can increase in knowledge of Him.

Compare Scripture on General Revelation

We can say the same with respect to the study of Scripture for what it teaches us about general revelation and how to understand and make use of it in a creational-theology mode. No single passage of God's Word can be definitive for teaching us how to discern the revelation of God in creation, culture, and the ways of men. Only as we gather more light, and compare passages with one another, will we be able to derive insights and principles that can guide our study of the works of God in general revelation.

Compare Studies in the Book of the World

But we can also say the same concerning our involvement with creation, culture, and the actions of conscience. Since God is revealing Himself in all these ways—revelation that can be discerned, understood, and put to good use only in the light of Scripture and the

173

gospel—we should expect to be able, by comparing what we observe in one area with what we observe in others, to assemble a better understanding of the line of God than if we simply listened to Him speaking in only one area. This is precisely what we see Edwards doing, for instance, when he compares the internal mechanisms of a clock with the motion of the planets and the turning of a chariot's wheel to help us in thinking about the way God is moving all things forward to history's final conclusion and the inauguration of the new heavens and new earth.

For example, we might conclude, by just observing the dress and antics of young people (the actions of their consciences), that God is speaking to us through what we see about the rebelliousness of today's youth. Yet we might arrive at a different conclusion if we were to talk with those young people, to spend time with them and get to know them; if we took the time to listen mindfully to their music; and if we could observe the effects of certain aspects of the culture on their lives— schools, television, broken homes, the frightening times in which we live, and so on. By comparing our involvement with general revelation in several areas, we might see that what God is revealing to us through today's youth is a cry of the heart for something meaningful, something safe, something that takes them seriously, and something that extends a welcome of love and acceptance to them.

So as we delight in the works of God in general revelation and begin to study them more deeply and carefully (Ps. 111:2), let us follow Edwards's second bit of advice about increasing in Christian knowledge and carefully study and compare our observations in the book of creation, culture, and the actions of conscience. It will be helpful, as we pursue these studies, to record our perceptions and experiences, perhaps in a journal or notebook, for later reflection and comparison with Scripture. Recording them in writing—similar to the journaling that we might do from our daily devotions, or that you have been doing in the Activity sections of each chapter of this book—gives us a permanent record that we can use to compare our observations in one area with those in another. This can lead to further observations and even preliminary conclusions as we further reflect on the line of God going out in the book of the world.

174

Consult the Experts

Third, Edwards advises us, "Procure, and diligently use, other books which may help you to grow in this knowledge."[11] Certainly this is excellent advice when it comes to the study of Scripture and sacred theology. No one will deny this. But we will find it equally valuable as we begin to study the book of general revelation.

Many Available Resources

Happily, many excellent resources are available, both from Christian writers and from those outside the community of faith, for beginning our study of creational theology. These latter materials will have to be read with particular care; yet many of them can inspire and enlighten us in surprising ways.

Wonderful resources are available to guide our studies in creation, culture, and the ways of men—books about the different aspects of creation and how to be in it; science and the arts; history and culture; and getting to know people.[12] Excellent tape series can also be procured from such sources as The Teaching Company. Ken Myers's *Mars Hill Audio Journal* is a very useful resource in thinking about matters of culture from a Christian point of view, as are the various resources available through the Wilberforce Forum of Prison Fellowship Ministries (including its Web page, BreakPoint.org). A variety of seminar and workshop opportunities are also available and can lead us to further resources and insights. Watch for ads about these in Christian periodicals, and consult the annotated bibliography at the end of this book for further guidance in selecting subjects for study.

Stay Close to Scripture

As with the use of all other secondary resources, we will want to make sure that our reading and study of books on general revelation is undertaken in the light of God's Word. In our efforts to improve our creational-theology skills, we must take care not to drift from our scriptural moorings, but always to examine any books we might read or courses we might attend and any conclusions we may be reaching in the light of the teaching of the Bible and sacred theology (Acts 17:11). If we can find room in our schedules for some reading and study of secondary sources, we may discover, as Edwards claimed, that they can "afford you a very profitable and pleasant entertainment in your leisure hours."[13]

Here again, we must expect to make some changes in the ways we use our time if we are going to benefit from the many excellent resources that are available to help us sharpen our creational-theology skills.

Converse with Others

Fourth, Edwards suggests that we will be more likely to grow in Christian knowledge and our understanding of sacred things if we take on this challenge in conversation with others:

> Improve conversation with others to this end. How much might persons promote each other's knowledge in divine things, if they would improve conversation as they might; if men that are ignorant were not ashamed to show their ignorance, and were willing to learn of others; if those that have knowledge would communicate it, without pride and ostentation; and if all were more disposed to enter on such conversation as would be for their mutual edification and instruction.[14]

Study with a Friend

Pursuing studies in general revelation in a creational-theology mode can be more interesting and rewarding—as well as more consistent—when they are done with others. This might be, for example, with just one other person. For a time my friend Robert Lynn, who lives in Ann Arbor, and I would meet together by telephone for half an hour or so every couple of weeks to discuss some works of John Polkinghorne on the interface between theology and science. My son Kevin and I have done the same with some studies in the history of philosophy. I have greatly benefited from my biweekly luncheons with Darren Hughes, a young man in our church, who has a particular interest in art and foreign films, with a view to discerning the line of God going out in this arena of general revelation. You may be able to find a friend who will read a book with you, go for an observation walk, or undertake some other study in the book of general revelation.

Start a Reading or Discussion Group

Starting a reading or discussion group for such a purpose is another possibility. In one church that I served, my wife and I held a monthly meeting that we called "Contours of Culture." In these meetings, which were open to anyone in the church, we discussed aspects of Western culture that we thought might help to inform us as to how people thought about God, religion, and the like. Our discussions of such subjects as Mozart's "Requiem" and the poetry of W. B. Yeats were very stimulating and helpful to many of the participants. In my present calling, the members of the teaching-group staff meet monthly to read and discuss books on Christian education. An arts group is also beginning to form for the purpose of considering how God would use our talents as artists to serve Him better. Many larger bookstores sponsor similar groups, although not with the intention of doing creational theology. Yet participating in a poetry circle, philosophy book group, or other kind of reading and discussion group that consists largely of unbelievers can be a wonderful opportunity for observation, personal growth, and reaching out with the gospel.

Discipline Your Conversations

Talking with one another or participating in a group discussion about our observations in the book of general revelation, or our readings in secondary sources, can help to make us more consistent in these studies. It can also provide a sounding board for our conclusions about what God may be showing us of Himself, His purposes, or His ways. If you have been doing the exercises in the Activity section at the end of each chapter, and if you have a conversation partner, you already know how enjoyable and rewarding such times of talking together can be. Friends can also help to keep us squarely grounded in the Word of God as we work through our study together. A very useful by-product of such a relationship is that we are disciplining our conversation, as well as our minds and hearts, to "think God's thoughts after Him" more and more. What we express in the course of such studies and discussions will inevitably shape what we say in other contexts—the conversations we have with people in our personal mission fields—thus helping to make our conversation overall more edifying and instructive.

Take It to Heart

Edwards, in his fifth recommendation, cautions against embarking on such studies merely for the sake of gaining knowledge with which we might impress others. Rather, he says, we should seek such knowledge "for the benefit of your souls, and in order to practice."[15] Our study of Scripture and sacred theology should reach not just to our minds but to our hearts, molding and shaping them for greater love for God and others. Out of such study—in our "practice"—should come heartfelt expressions of love to God, in the form of worship and service, and love to others, in caring for them, speaking to them of God and His greatness, and meeting their needs.

Keep Your Purpose in Mind

So also with our studies in the book of general revelation. Our purpose is not just to learn new things with which to impress others, whether saved or lost. Our purpose is to grow in the knowledge of God and to be more conformed to the image of Christ from the heart. If doing creational theology does not lead to growth in love, then we have missed the point of the exercise altogether (1 Tim. 1:5). In each of our studies, therefore, it will be good to be constantly asking ourselves, How does this help me to love the Lord more? To love others better? To serve them more effectively? What will I do with what I am learning in order to show the Lord and my neighbor that I love them? As I have suggested, you may find it helpful as you undertake these various studies to keep a journal where you can record your activities, observations, and conclusions. A journal can also be a place for setting forth resolutions as to how what you are learning will affect your behavior toward God and others. This was Edwards's own practice over the years of his life.

Take Time to Worship

Recall the words of Cowper at the beginning of this chapter:

Happy who walks with him! whom what he finds
Of flavor or of scent in fruit or flower,
Of what he views of beautiful or grand
In nature, from the broad majestic oak
To the green blade that twinkles in the sun,
Prompts with remembrance of a present God.
His presence, who made all so fair, perceived,
Makes all fairer still.

Let what you perceive and experience lead you to spontaneous expressions of worship: praise for the creation, thanksgiving for the many gifts of God revealed in culture, intercession for the lost over the hardness of their hearts, and so forth. Bring worship into your studies and daily activities as you encounter the presence of God and His glorious line going out in all the things He has made. I can think of no better way of taking to heart your sorties into the book of the world than by acknowledging, worshiping, and appealing to Him who made these fair things, and makes them fairer still as we discover Him in them.

Look to God

"Seek to God, that he would direct you, and bless you, in this pursuit after knowledge."[16] Edwards's sixth recommendation is perhaps the most important of all. In all our studies, all our disciplined pursuit of the knowledge of God—whether in special or general revelation—we must be careful to seek the Lord in prayer. There we can wait upon Him to illumine our minds with understanding, fill our hearts with wonder and love, and show us ways to put our learning into practice.

For Humility

In prayer we can ask the Lord to give us humility, check any inclinations toward pride, and remind us that the more we learn, the more we will discover how much remains to learn of Him. Prayer can make all our studies adventures in wonder and worship, and provide a context for ever-increasing, specific praise and thanks to our self-revealing God.

For Meditation on the New Heavens and New Earth

As we will see in the next chapter, in prayer we can also meditate on the glories of the new heaven and the new earth, where, completed in glory and continuously in the presence of the Lord, we will know the full blessings of His self-disclosing ways in the perfection of His Spirit and of our heavenly dwelling place. Such times of sweet reflection, praise, and wonder in prayer will carry over into our worship of God at other times, greatly enriching all we do to celebrate the majesty, greatness, grace, mercy, and wonder of our glorious God and Savior.

For Guidance in Serving Others

And seek God in prayer that He might show you how to use what you are learning about Him and His purposes, ways, and truth to reach out more effectively to others with His grace. We must not take up this task as an end in itself. God's revelation in creation, culture, and the acts of conscience reveals His glory, which the Spirit of God can use to mold us more perfectly into the image of Jesus Christ (2 Cor. 3:18). As Jesus used God's general revelation to proclaim the kingdom and mercies of God, so must we. But this attitude and ability will come only as we take our studies and other kinds of involvement in the book of the world to our loving, equipping God in prayer.

Studying and Doing

Finally, Edwards recommends, "Practise according to what knowledge you have. This will be the way to know more."[17] Learning is com-

180

plete only when it is put into practice—whether in praise to God, amendment of our lives, or service to others. Any efforts to learn to do creational theology that do not result in meaningful life change are incomplete. We must diligently seek the Lord to discover what He would have us do with the things we are learning, how He wants us to put into practice the things He is showing us in the book of general revelation. The conclusions we reach, which we perhaps record in our journal, we should diligently implement with care and consistency, pursuing holiness in the Lord in all things (2 Cor. 7:1). For merely *knowing* what we should do is of no benefit unless we actually *do* it, as the apostle James reminds us (James 1:22–25).

A world of wonder, excitement, and insight into the ways of God awaits us in the things God has made. Jonathan Edwards certainly labored to acquire the ability to read the book of general revelation, and he made good use of what he learned there in his ministry in Northampton. His example, together with his recommendations, can enhance our efforts to know the Lord and deepen our sense of happiness in Him. As Cowper reminds us, God's presence in the works of His hands—the creation around us, and the cultures and ways of men—is the only explanation for so much that is beautiful, good, and true in general revelation. Yet developing the ability to perceive and experience that presence, to discern the line of God going out in the things He has made, makes general revelation "fairer still" and can be for us a source of increasing joy and sanctification in the Lord.

Questions for Study or Discussion

1. Which aspects of Edwards's advice about entering into the task of creational theology seem most interesting and promising to you? Why?

2. Can you think of some people you might invite to join you in this effort? What form might that take? How would you begin to get organized?

3. Look at your own week-in, week-out experiences—the places you go, people you meet, and responsibilities you fulfill. What do these experiences suggest about some topics or subject matter to begin your studies in creational theology? How do you hope your studies will help to equip you for loving God and your neighbors more fully?

4. Do you have the time for this undertaking? Will you need to adjust your schedule in any ways in order to improve your use of time for the purposes of creational theology? In what ways?

5. Well, are you making progress toward your goals for this study? Why or why not? Where will you go from here?

The Happy Task of Creational Theology

Activity 7

Review each of Edwards's seven recommendations for growing in the knowledge of God. Choose one in which to begin making significant progress, starting right away. What will you do? What specific steps will you take in the next few days to help ensure that you are "opening the book of the world" with greater care and consistency? Write them in your notebook or on a separate sheet of paper.

Go through this exercise for each of the other six recommendations as well, until you have laid out the parameters of a personal plan for making better use of God's general revelation through the disciplines of creational theology.

PRACTICING CREATIONAL THEOLOGY (2): CIRCLING 'ROUND THE CREATOR

> *For with thee is the fountain of life:*
> *in thy light shall we see light.*
> —Psalm 36:9

> *A Calvinist who seeks God, does not for a moment think of*
> *limiting himself to theology and contemplation, leaving the*
> *other sciences, as of a lower character, in the hands of unbe-*
> *lievers; but on the contrary, looking upon it as his task to*
> *know God in* all *his works, he is conscious of having been*
> *called to fathom with all the energy of his intellect, things ter-*
> *restrial as well as things celestial; to open to view both the*
> *order of creation, and the "common grace" of the God he*
> *adores, in nature and its wondrous character, in the produc-*
> *tion of human industry, in the life of mankind, in sociology*
> *and in the history of the human race.*
> —Abraham Kuyper[1]

Let me be to thee as the circling bird,
Or bat with tender and air-crisping wings
That shapes in half-light his departing rings,
From both of whom a changeless note is heard.

I have found my music in a common word,
Trying each pleasurable throat that sings
And every praiséd sequence of sweet strings,
And know infallibly which I preferred.

The authentic cadence was discovered late
Which ends those only strains that I approve,
And other science all gone out of date
And minor sweetness scarce made mention of:
I have found the dominant of my range and state—
Love, O my God, to call Thee Love and Love.

—*Gerard Manley Hopkins*

For Hopkins, poetry, though entered upon relatively late in life, was the "dominant chord" of his existence. Though he was a Jesuit priest, a pastor, and an educator, he believed that his most significant song would be sung to the praises of the God he loved so dearly through the machinations and images of verse—"a common word." He intended each of his poems to be a sacrifice of praise to God. This was to be his "changeless note." And for this to be the case, he knew he had to "circle 'round" God, keeping a close orbit to Him, letting all other study and every other occupation be of secondary importance to increasing in the knowledge of God and love for Him. Thus he was a deeply spiritual man, devoted to an ascetic life that included much study and reflection on the Word of God, seasons of solitude and meditation, and frequent prayer.

If we are not equally diligent, our studies in the book of the world can lead us away from God or, at least, can diminish our love for God and see it replaced by a greater interest in and devotion to the things He has made. So beautiful, wondrous, and diverse are the glories to be perceived and experienced in "things terrestrial" that they can easily engage our affections with great power. This can lead us to avocations that can become obsessions when we begin to spend more time in them and thinking about them than we do with the Lord and thinking about Him. But this would be idolatry, of which none of us wants to be found guilty. Therefore, we must each be diligent, as we take up the happy task of creational theology, to ensure that our studies lead us to increased love for God and others. As Alister McGrath advises, "The New Testament does not present us with a worked-out theology of creation, but provides a series of statements concerning creation which require creation to be viewed in a Christologically focused and trinitarian manner."[2] Otherwise, we will have missed the point of God's general revelation altogether. Therefore, we must be careful to circle 'round the Creator, continually immersing ourselves in "things celestial," in all we do and at all times.

We have already touched on this point in the preceding chapter. In this chapter I simply want to recommend some ways of helping to ensure that as we "turn with care" the pages of the book of the world, we will continue circling 'round the Creator, so that our work in creational theology might truly result in learning to love Him, to call Him love, and to love others in His name. Doing so will help us to gain the benefit that God intends for us from His general revelation—improved worship and progress in our sanctification. It seems fitting for a discussion of such goals to include a note of exhortation, encouraging us to abide in Christ, abide in His agenda, and abide in our promised hope.

Abide in Christ

Abide in me, and I in you. As the branch cannot bear fruit of itself, except it abide in the vine; no more can ye, except ye abide in me. I am the vine, ye are the branches: He that abideth in me, and I in him, the same bringeth forth much fruit: for without me ye can do nothing. (John 15:4-5)

Everything that we do in the life of faith must be undertaken within this framework: we are to abide in Christ and in His Word, so that we might be fruitful for Him. For those who have come to know Jesus Christ, all that they are and do is in the context of a deeply personal relationship with Him who gave His life that we might live. In such a relationship the overall inclination of our hearts must be gratitude and worship, followed by a desire to please our Lord, in whom we find such peace, joy, and delight. As we take up the happy task of creational theology, therefore, and all the disciplines of it, we must labor to make certain that we are abiding in the Lord, circling 'round the Redeemer/Creator at all times. As Stanley Hauerwas reminds us, our work in the field of general revelation will bear fruit only to the extent that it is focused on the work of Jesus Christ for our salvation.[3] By ensuring, in our work of creational theology, that we are abiding in Christ at all times, we can have reason to hope that our perceptions and experiences in this exciting area of theological studies might bear the fruit of worship and sanctification He desires for us.

Abide in His Word

This means, in the first place, increasing and improving our study of and reflection on the Word of God. Only in the light of Scripture will we be able to make sense out of and appreciate the profound messages of creation, culture, and the actions of conscience. Scripture teaches us how to perceive and experience these things in a manner consistent with God's purposes in revealing Himself there. It teaches us the questions to ask, the principles we may derive, and the limits to which we may draw conclusions from our observations. So as we continue developing our skills in the practice of creational theology, we must be equally diligent in paying attention to what the Bible teaches us about this area of theological studies.

In addition, embarking on a program of creational theology should be an impetus to improving mastery of the skills involved in *biblical* theology—the skills of exegesis, interpretation, and application of God's Word to our daily lives. We will want to learn how to read and understand the different genre of Scripture; to employ the analogy of Scripture in comparing texts; and to recognize and avoid those mistakes in exegesis that can lead us down blind alleys or around wrong turns.

Further, we will want to make sure that we are increasing our grasp of the whole counsel of God in the Bible (Acts 20:27). We must set a course to become more familiar with all the books of the Bible, as well as with the unfolding story of redemption and restoration that God is revealing there. We must resolve to strengthen our understanding of familiar and beloved books and press on to gain a higher level of mastery over less familiar parts of Scripture. This will mean more time in study of the Word, in learning to listen more carefully to preaching and teaching, and in taking part in study groups and courses that can help us to become better stewards over the whole counsel of God.

Finally, we will want to improve our ability to see Christ in all of Scripture (John 5:39). The Bible—indeed, all the revelation of God—is pointing us to Jesus, so that we might see the glory of God revealed in His face and be drawn through Him to greater love for God and others (2 Cor. 4:6). We must become more adept at handling the Word of truth (2 Tim. 2:15) and increase our overall understanding of the story of the Bible and the message of its several parts. And we must seek to draw ever closer to Jesus in worship and discipleship as a result of our studies. This will put us in good stead to perceive and experience the revelation of God in creation, culture, and the actions of the human conscience.

Active involvement in the work of creational theology will only confuse and disappoint us if we neglect, or fail to improve, our study of God's Word. Biblical theology is the "big picture window" of theological studies. The better we become at learning to see through this clearest and most central window of glory, the better we will be able to discern what God is showing us through the window of creational theology.

Abide in His World

We must also learn to abide in the Lord more consistently in all our daily activities, keeping in mind that, at all times, we live and move and have our being in God and in His world (Acts 17:28; Ps. 24:1). The Lord Jesus Christ is with us always (Matt. 28:20), ever ready to commune with us over the revelation of His glory in the things He has made. The apostle Paul's exhortation to "pray without ceasing" (1 Thess. 5:17) is not idle rhetoric. He means for us to cultivate a conversational relationship with the living God, and to take every opportunity to converse with Him over the glory we experience in our environment, our relationships, our vocations, our diversions, and the

187

ordinary events of everyday life, and to listen as He communes with us concerning His glory.[4]

Let things wondrous or beautiful lead you to contemplate the beauty and majesty of Christ, enthroned at the right hand of the Father. Allow tragedies, disappointments, and the everyday sufferings and sorrows of our fellow human beings to find you bowing before the throne of grace to reaffirm your trust in the sovereign goodness and power of God. Let glad times lead to greater rejoicing in the Lord. Improve stewardship in all your relationships, roles, and responsibilities, knowing that it is the Lord you serve, and not men (Col. 3:23–24). Take every opportunity to season your conversation with grace, and to edify those around you who have been made in the image of God (Col. 4:6; Eph. 4:29).

In other words, make a point of becoming mindful of the fact that you and all the people, places, and things of your life belong to Jesus Christ, and practice abiding in Him—through reflection, meditation, and prayer—as you move about in His world.

Abide in Worship

Finally, make worship a deeper, richer, and more continual part of your walk with the Lord. We have been redeemed by the Lord to worship Him (Ps. 100). It is our reasonable worship to live our everyday lives in an attitude and the practices of giving thanks and praise to God (Rom. 12:1–2). Our work in the area of creational theology can be a great enhancement to these purposes, but we must consciously undertake this lifestyle with greater consistency and depth.

Pay attention during public worship to the ways that creational theology intrudes there. In sermon illustrations, lines from hymns, and the music of choirs, for instance, make a point to note the use of creational theology—whether done consciously or otherwise—and use some of the Lord's Day to reflect on these uses and how they can improve your worship and sanctification. The old hymns of the church are rich with allusions and images that can provoke us to deeper reflection on the glory of God in the book of the world.[5] Then take those hymns with you into your daily life, where singing them will lead to reflection and worship amid the routines and responsibility of family and work.

Abide in Christ's Agenda

> And I say also unto thee, That thou art Peter, and upon this rock I will build my church; and the gates of hell shall not prevail against it. (Matt. 16:18)

If our work in the area of creational theology ends up benefiting only ourselves, we will have fallen short of the agenda Christ proclaimed for His work in these latter days. He is laboring to build His church, to raise up a body, a community of people knitted together in love, combining their voices in worship and their skills in mission to advance the kingdom of God and further the presence of His glory on earth, as it is in heaven. As we craft our own peculiar songs in this area, therefore, we need to keep this agenda in mind and consider ways that we might, as we abide in Christ, ensure that we are also abiding in His agenda. This will mean continuing to apply ourselves to the tasks of growing in grace, building up the body of Christ, and reaching out to the lost with the good news of God's love and forgiveness.

Grow in Grace

All our theological studies are part of the grand effort of growing in grace and in the knowledge of our Lord and Savior, Jesus Christ (2 Peter 3:18). This is no less true of the happy task of creational theology. We should expect our time spent gazing through this window of glory to yield greater growth in grace in at least two areas.

1. First, we should expect to become more eager and adept at seeking the Lord (Ps. 63:1–2; 105:4). As we take up studies in creation, culture, and the actions of conscience, we will find that we are already about this most fundamental aspect of what it means to grow in grace. We are seeking the Lord and His glory, to know Him, to discover insights into His purposes, ways, and truth, and to reflect in loving worship on our observations there. Creational theology must not be an end in itself; rather, it is a means to get at God's general revelation so that we may improve worship of God and sanctification in His grace and truth. We do not merely seek to understand the creation; we seek

189

the Lord there. We must not be content simply to admire the products of culture; we want to discover the Lord's hand behind the work of His image-bearers. Our studies in human actions, which are expressions of their consciences in everyday practices, are done so that we might see the truth of God and His purposes played out in the arena of human life. Be careful always to look beyond the subject of your study. Seek the Lord, observe His glory there, and then pursue Him in worship as you circle 'round Him in loving gratitude and wonder at the works of His hand.

2. Growing in grace also entails delighting in the Lord. The beauty of a work of art is but a reflection of the beauty of Christ. The intricacy and wonder of a leaf should speak to us of the details of God's lovingkindness and delight us with the thought of His continuously working to hold together all the intricate details of our own physical existence. Delighting in the Lord means telling Him how astonished we are at the "utter regularity of it all." It will find us joyfully singing praises to the Lord, and talking excitedly with others about our encounters with His glory through the window of creational theology. Often, when we have had a particularly enjoyable experience, we memorialize it in some way—taking pictures and storing them in an album to share with others, for example. The poetry I write in response to my studies in creational theology gives me enormous joy, both in taming the forms and devices of the poet's craft to express my sentiments and beliefs and also in having something to share with others, thus making my own contribution to God's general revelation through an artifact of culture. Each poem is for me a kind of benchmark of growth. Reading them over again, I experience anew the delight I felt in the initial observation, as well as the joy of reading and sharing what I have written. And this leads me to praise and thanksgiving, deeper delight in the Lord, and growth in His wondrous grace and truth.

Such seeking the Lord and delighting in Him has a way of encouraging more of the same. The pleasure we find in the work of creational theology will be fully realized only as we actually come to better know the Lord and His grace, reinforcing our experiences and conclusions from the areas of biblical and spiritual theology, and preparing us for

190

the work of practical theology as we turn from personal growth to the work of making disciples and building the church.

Building Up the Body of Christ

Second, we abide in the Lord's agenda as we apply the lessons of theological study to the task of ministering God's grace to others, with a view to strengthening the body of Christ. I strongly recommend that your studies in creational theology eventuate in some *product* that seeks to capture your experience and perceptions—whether photographs, a journal, a poem or painting, or just a time of conversation with others about what you have learned. Let others benefit from what God is showing you; let the growth He is bringing into your life spill out and over into theirs, as the Spirit of God declares and shows His glory in refreshing deeds and words of grace to others (John 7:37–39). Whatever your ministry may be in the local church—whether teaching, singing in the choir, visiting the sick, counseling the confused, serving as an officer, or serving in any other capacity—bring the fruit of your labors in creational theology to bear on the work of ministry to which the Lord has called you.

The church of Christ is built up as God's people grow in grace and devote themselves in love to one another and to the lost, each joint and sinew being strengthened and working to capacity for the building up of the body in love (Eph. 4:11–16). Whatever growth in grace the Lord brings to you through your labors in the happy task of creational theology must not be spent on yourself alone. Take what you have learned into the work that helps to fulfill the agenda of our Lord Jesus Christ, that of building up His body to the praise of the glory of His grace.

Seek the Lost

Finally, and as I have just suggested, we abide in the Lord's agenda as we apply His truth to the task of reaching the lost. We are called to be witnesses for Jesus Christ (Acts 1:8). Whatever it takes for us to communicate the good news of Jesus to the people around us, the Lord Himself will supply (Phil. 4:13, 19). But we must determine to become

191

equipped for reaching people at the point of their ability to hear the good news (1 Cor. 9:19–23). And creational theology can be of much help to us in this endeavor.

Consider the people to whom the Lord has sent you as His ambassador (John 20:21; 2 Cor. 5:20). What are their interests? What subjects, activities, or diversions command their devotion? How much do you know about these things? Enough to discover the glory of God in them, and to help your friends consider what He might be showing them of Himself there? Consider how skillfully our Lord Jesus turned a woman's focus on water to the necessity of the very Water of Life (John 4). Or how Paul took pagan Greek poetry captive and made it obedient to the task of proclaiming the good news of Christ to a society of philosophers in Athens (2 Cor. 10:3–5; Acts 17). Our Lord and His apostles understood the times and the concerns of those around them, and they knew what they had to do to make the gospel intelligible to the lost, so that the elect among them might see the light of truth (1 Chron. 12:32).

Can we say the same? That baseball fanatic at the office; or that woman consumed with staying fit and trim; the colleague who lives for fly-fishing; the party guy who knows all the latest tunes; the neighbor who spends all her free time working in her yard and garden; that friend who can't wait to see the latest new movie—can we discern where, in any of these activities, the Lord might be revealing Himself, and are we able to talk with people about His glory in a language they might readily understand and be willing to hear? These things may not be of interest to us; but if we are to be all things to all people, in order that we might be used to bring some of them to a saving knowledge of Christ (1 Cor. 9:19–23), then we must make at least some effort to learn how to communicate with them at the point of their interest, being careful to avoid falling into the sins that affect them so. This is a truth that every person preparing for cross-cultural missions understands well. Do we apply it to our own mission in the Lord's service, for the sake of building up His body and completing His agenda?

Creational theology can serve us well as we carry out our calling as witnesses for Christ. It can provide abundant new angles and colors of light to introduce into our conversations about the gospel of Jesus Christ, light that just may open up a fissure to some chosen one's heart. Let us take up this discipline, therefore, with a view to becoming better equipped to proclaim the message of salvation to the lost. Thus the church will be built up, as the Lord uses what He shows us of Himself in creation, culture, and the actions of conscience to enable us to reach out to others in their own "tongue" and according to their own unique passions and concerns.

Abide in Hope

> In my Father's house are many mansions: if it were not so, I would have told you. I go to prepare a place for you. And if I go and prepare a place for you, I will come again, and receive you unto myself; that where I am, there ye may be also. (John 14:2–3)

Finally, as we develop our ability to gaze through the window of creational theology, let what we discern and discover there be for us a constant stimulus to hope. As Barry Morrow reminds us, "God has provided 'signals of transcendence' in our everyday lives that hint of another world to come."[6] Let the messages of glory conveyed through creation, culture, and the actions of conscience remind us of God's steadfast love and faithfulness, His presence with us always, and His promise of a new heavens and new earth where glory dwell.

As you take up the disciplines of creational theology, cultivate the hope of seeing God's glory, of knowing His presence, and of seeing into our eternal hope and glory. To nurture such hope, we must persevere in this work of creational theology. Further, we must practice, in conjunction with the disciplines of creational theology, those disciplines of spiritual and biblical theology that can help us to sense the presence of God in the things we perceive and experience. Finally, I want to encourage you to apply your observations and conclusions from the work of creational theology to projecting for yourself and others a clearer vision of our eternal hope and heavenly home.

193

Of Seeing His Line Going Out: Persevere!

In the first place, then, in order that we might abide in hope as a result of our labors in creational theology, let us resolve to take up this task for the long haul. Creational theology is hard work. It can be frustrating and confusing; it can lead to uncertainty about what we are observing, or leave us speechless, though filled with awe and wonder. We do not expect to master the revelation of God in Scripture without learning the skills and disciplines necessary to look through this window of glory, or without devoting our entire lives (part of every day) to reading, studying, and contemplating God in His Word. Creational theology is no different. God is truly speaking to us through the things He has made, as we have seen (Ps. 19:1–6). But it pleases Him for us to have to work at perceiving and experiencing Him there, that as we ferret out His glory, our labors will bring us the satisfaction, delight, and sanctification He desires for us.

So don't get discouraged. Keep at it. As Richard Mouw advises us, "We cannot give up on the important task—which the theologians of common grace have correctly urged upon us—of actively working to discern God's complex designs in the midst of our deeply wounded world."[7] Work at honing your skills in whatever fields of creation, culture, or the actions of conscience you choose to labor. Keep records, and talk with others. Seek the Lord in prayer in all your work, crying out to Him to make Himself and His glory known. He will surely do so, for His desire in so revealing Himself is that we might know and worship Him and be helped in our sanctification and calling. Realize that the voice telling you such things as "This is too hard for you," or "You're never going to get it," or "God is not speaking through such things as this," or "This is a labor for experts," is not the voice of the Lord. Banish all such thoughts and believe that each of us, just like Hopkins, Cowper, Edwards, and all the others we have seen in the preceding pages, can know joyous, even life-changing encounters with God's glory through the things He has made. Keep this hope alive as you circle 'round the Lord and His general revelation.

194

Of Knowing His Presence: Practice!

It will take a little doing to be able to consistently experience the presence of God in your studies. Not in every case: walking a mountain trail or surveying a beautiful landscape from a commanding height, contemplating some extraordinary work of sacrifice or love, or listening to a Bach cantata will certainly bring us into the presence of God in ways that can affect us greatly, even lastingly. But what about in the daily drudgery of reading and studying, perceiving and experiencing, listening and conversing that makes up the disciplines of creational theology? Let me make three suggestions.

1. *Know what you're looking for.* It will be difficult to discern when we have come into the presence of God unless we know what we're looking for. Jacob was surprised to discover that he was in the presence of God (Gen. 28:10–16). His experience at Bethel can help us know what to look for when once we have come into the presence of God. As I experience it, and as I think I see it here in this passage, being in the presence of God means, first, that some word of God comes immediately to my mind (vv. 13–15). That sparrow crashing against my plate-glass window and lying on my deck immediately led me to think of Jesus' comment about sparrows falling and God's compassion for them as they do (Matt. 10:29). As I went to the window and looked out on him, gasping there on the deck, I couldn't help repeating that verse over and over in my mind, and thinking beyond that verse to other passages related to the sovereignty of God's Word over all things (cf. Ps. 104). The more I looked and considered the little bird's plight, and the more I meditated on God's Word, the more I began to be aware of His closeness to me in this situation.

2. *Commune with God according to His Word.* As I rushed outside and lifted that little dying bird into my hand, for some reason I kept thinking of Christ sovereignly upholding the universe and all things in it according to His good, albeit mysterious, purposes and pleasure (Col. 1:17; Heb. 1:1–3). I found myself praying for that little bird, and marveling before the Lord in prayer at the wonder and majesty of His ways on earth (Ps. 8). Jacob did not directly pray in this passage. But his vow to give the Lord a tenth of all he earned, because of what he

trusted would be the Lord's goodness to him, is itself a form of prayer that served to reinforce the presence of God with Jacob. As you are perceiving the glory of God around you, your ability to experience His presence there will be heightened by your entering into conversation with Him concerning the things you are observing through the window of creational theology.

3. *Let the wonder, beauty, awe, or might of God catch you up from within; then create some expression of your experience of the divine presence.* I don't know how to put this other than to say, let yourself *feel* the presence of God, and all the fear, wonder, excitement, and hope that comes with His presence. Then find some way to express that feeling that will enable you to recall it or share it with someone else. Jacob's voice at Bethel sounds filled with excitement and hope, humility and determination. He had *experienced* something—God's presence—that affected him mightily. The altar he erected memorialized both his encounter with God and his vow. We should expect the same to be the case—to a greater or lesser degree—as we encounter the glory of God through the disciplines of creational theology. In the case of this dying bird, my sense of God's presence was heightened as I meditated on life and death, the cycle of the seasons, and the power and goodness of God undergirding it all. I can recall shuddering with fear in the presence of such might, yet at the same time thrilling with joy and hope to know that this power is constantly at work for my good (Matt. 10:30–31; Rom. 8:28). I wanted, like Jacob erecting that pillar (Gen. 28:18–19), to memorialize that experience, to have something to share with Susie and others, and to be able—again, like Jacob—to revisit that experience of God's presence as often as I may (Gen. 35). The poem that opens this section brings that entire experience and the Word and promises of God, as well as His presence, back to me afresh each time I read it. You may not write a poem, but a photograph, a journal entry, a sketch, or just a conversation with a fellow observer can help to heighten your sense of the divine presence, and allow you to recall that experience and share it with others.

Of Seeing into Our Eternal Hope and Glory: Project!

Finally, cultivate the hope, as you experience the glory of God through the things He has made, of what He has laid up for us in eternal glory in the new heavens and new earth. For now, we see but dimly the glory, greatness, and goodness of God—even in the bright light of His general and special revelation (1 Cor. 13:12). But a day is coming in which what is now but dimly visible will be gloriously illuminated without obstruction, hindrance, or end. Let your work of creational theology begin to build up a vision in your heart of faith concerning what that final estate will be like.

Creational theology can help your understanding of biblical texts that talk about the estate of glory. As we learn to perceive God's glory and experience His presence, we will take new excitement into the reading and study of such passages as Revelation 21 and 22. We will be better able to anticipate what is there imaged for us, and we will find that God's Word comes alive with new brilliance to enrich our intellectual understanding of the glory that is to come.

We will also find our affections stirred as we think about the new heavens and the new earth. We live in a day when, for most believers, their enthusiasm about the faith of Jesus Christ revolves mostly around what they think He can do for them here and now. We are not a people much given to contemplation on, or excitement about, the prospect of going to heaven.[8] But many believers have found that their confidence, boldness, and joy in the present is greatly expanded by being able to think clearly and broadly about the life to come, and actually to experience that hope with greater joy and assurance.

The glory we encounter through the disciplines of creational theology is but a foretaste of the banquet of glory that is stored up for us in the new heavens and the new earth. As we nibble on the sweet but comparatively meager offerings that God serves up to us at this time, let them be for us a hint of what is yet to come—appetizers of an unending feast of glory that is even now being prepared for us. Let your imagination and affections wander into sweet revelry—in meditation, prayer, or singing—as you see more intently and clearly into the life to come, and hope for it more fully. Project for yourself and others a rich, glorious, thrilling vision of the new heavens and new earth, and know that as you do, even that exciting vision is but a dimly lit foreshadowing of the infinitely more glorious and wondrous hope that is stored up for us with Jesus!

Circling Birds, All

"Let me be to thee as the circling bird . . ." Every believer in Jesus Christ is a frail sparrow, circling 'round the infinite majesty and glory of God, sustained in all our utter regularity by His might and invited into His presence for sweet communion, worship, and renewing grace. God alone can make our lives richer, more filled with wonder and satisfaction, more characterized by worship and fraught with power for serving others. He accomplishes this in us by communicating Himself to us, in the Person of His Holy Spirit, through the means of His glory revealed by the Book of the Word and the book of the world. Our calling is to seek the Lord and to "find the dominant" of our "range and state" so that we might sing choruses of praise and live symphonies of gratitude to Him. His Word is the principal light through which we come to know this kind of life (John 6:63; Ps. 36:9).

But the light and line of God going out through the things He has made—in creation, culture, and the actions of conscience—can offer much help as we seek the Lord and His purpose for our lives. As diligently as we work to come into the light of Scripture, therefore, let us begin, with equal diligence, to be daily bathed in the glory-filled light of the world God has made. Let us take up with determination, gladness, anticipation, and great hope the happy task of creational theology. And let us concentrate in all our endeavors on celebrating, declaring, and manifesting the glory of Him who deigns to show Himself to us through the works of His hand.

Questions for Study or Discussion

1. How might you begin to incorporate some awareness of creational theology into your daily devotional life with the Lord?

2. In which of the areas mentioned in this chapter—abiding in Christ, abiding in His agenda, abiding in hope—do you need to be strengthened? How might taking up the task of creational theology help?

3. How would you assess the activities you have been involved in thus far in the work of creational theology? Have they helped to improve your relationship with God? In what ways?

4. What kinds of "theological products" are you inclined to create from your work in creational theology? How might you use them in helping to build up the body of Christ?

5. Review the goals you set for this study at the end of chapter 1. Are you making progress in realizing these goals?

The Happy Task of Creational Theology

Activity 8

Spend some time reviewing your journal entries thus far. In a paragraph or two, summarize what you have learned about the Lord from these activities. How have your labors in creational theology thus far helped you to grow in knowledge of the Lord and of His purposes, truth, and ways?

Now, what might you produce to share these conclusions with others? A poem? A brief talk? An illustration for teaching? A sketch or song? Create your own "theological product"!

9

DOCENTS OF GLORY

O sing unto the LORD *a new song: sing unto the* LORD, *all
the earth. Sing unto the* LORD, *bless his name; shew forth
his salvation from day to day. Declare his glory among the
heathen, his wonders among all people.*
—Psalm 96:1–3

*Man abuses nature most rudely when he fails to find
in it a pedestal to praise God and be grateful to Him.*
—Stanley Jaki[1]

I had arrived early for a meeting in suburban Philadelphia. So with
a couple of hours to spare, I stopped by the Brandywine River Museum
in Chadds Ford for a cup of coffee and some time in the Andrew Wyeth
gallery on the third floor. Although my purpose was only to kill time,
I could not have anticipated the joyous encounter with the living God
that would ensue on that snowy afternoon.

I was admiring a new Wyeth landscape, one of his typically beautiful representations of the Pennsylvania countryside, marveling at the
fact that here is this man, well into his 80s, still toiling away at the
thing for which he was put on earth, and doing so with as much skill

201

and beauty as ever. I was studying the details of the painting when one of the museum docents came alongside. I said, "He's amazing, isn't he? Still so much beauty and wonder." To which she replied, "You should have been here two days ago." "Oh?" I asked. "Yes," she continued, "Mr. Wyeth came up here with his paints to do some work on this painting." "Here? In the museum?" "Yes. See, right here" (she pointed to a place along a fence bordering a growth of brush) "he painted out a deer. He said he felt the presence of the deer would be much more powerful if he merely left the suggestion of it rather than the actual image, so he just painted it out."

I was thrilled, for I was immediately put in mind of Wyeth's penchant for just this sort of thing—establishing the presence of an object more by intimation than representation. He often does this in his paintings, by hints and lines and images as diverse as hills, a bucket, or a dinner bell suggesting the presence of someone or something that has special meaning for him. You can understand and appreciate what he is doing only if you take the time to study his work and learn something about his purposes and ways in painting. Suddenly that painting came alive for me in a new way. The *hint* of a deer affected me more powerfully than if the deer were actually present in the painting. Its absence provoked me to imagine Wyeth himself in that field, the many people and creatures he must have imagined or seen there, the history of the place (an aspect of the Brandywine region that much enthralls Andrew Wyeth), and the special times he had spent throughout his life wandering those fields and hills.

Filled with wonder and admiration, and thanking God for the gifts He had given to Andrew Wyeth, I went downstairs to the coffee shop, purchased a cup of coffee, and took a table near the window overlooking the Brandywine River. I began to meditate and make some notes on my experience. At length I noticed that the people around me were all whispering excitedly and pointing across the river to the snow-covered bank on the other side. A red fox was stealing in and out of the brush, offering occasional glimpses of living beauty against the pristine background of the white, wintry ground cover. Here we were in an art museum that held the works of one of America's finest living artists, and what everyone was excited about was the work of the divine Artist unfolding on the snowy bank. Here was "natural" beauty—the beauty of what struck me as unspoiled, almost Edenic creation—carrying on its normal routine before our eyes, and we were all amazed, hungry to participate in it. Now my mind began to race as I became caught up in the excitement of the other visitors. God was competing with Andrew Wyeth, and winning hands down, I mused. It's one thing to get excited about the beauty of culture, of a work carefully crafted to depict an ideal beauty that only few of us can ever reproduce. It's another thing to stumble on the beauty of God's glory unfolding quite casually around us. I wanted to remember this afternoon—the new Wyeth painting, his devotion to his calling, the sudden snowfall, the excitement of seeing the fox, the wonder I experienced over the excitement of the people who seemed to be caught up in the presence of living beauty, the beauty of creation, and what all this might imply about me and the people with me in that café. I wrote the following poem to clarify my experience and meditations, and to preserve them for future reliving:

Longing for Eden (at the Brandywine River Museum)

The sudden snow drops down upon the valley of
the Brandywine in sanctifying wafers. All
is purified in minutes, like a Christmas ball
a child shakes. In the conservancy café above
the river, culture-seekers, resting from our love
of art, relax, refresh, and watch the snow that falls
in silent glory all around. Behind our wall
of tinted glass we gaze in wonder at the dove-
like downpour, white and pure and holy. Something moves
across the river: In the snowy brush a small
red fox pursues his business, unaware of all
the eyes and pointing fingers and the whispers of
"Oh, there he is!" as we peer into the pristine wood
to catch a glimpse of something pure, unspoiled, and good.

For me, this is what creational theology is all about. Even as I read this poem again I'm caught up in the wonder, the joy, and the praise

203

of God, who visits us with such sudden beauty, calling us to consider, embrace, and know Him. As those who have covenanted with our eyes to perceive and experience the revelation of God in creation, culture, and the actions of conscience, we have a special calling, a high and glorious duty to fulfill on behalf of our fellow human beings, a calling and duty that can be greatly aided through the disciplines of creational theology. We are called to be docents of glory.

My friend Jim Greeley is a docent at the Baltimore Museum of Art. He spends time each week wandering through the galleries, chatting with visitors, pointing out aspects of this or that work of art that they might not have noticed, helping them to perceive and experience the work more carefully, so as to appreciate its beauty more fully. In order to do this, Jim has to know something about the artists exhibited at the BMA and about the particular works of art on display there. So he studies in order to familiarize himself with their works, to experience and appreciate them for himself, and to develop his skills at leading others to perceive and experience the wonder and beauty of each artist and his or her work.

This is precisely what we are called to do concerning the revelation of God in creation, culture, and the actions of conscience. God has appointed us docents in His museum of wonders and glory, and charged us with declaring His glory to one and all, pointing out the beauty, goodness, truth, wonder, majesty, power, and lovingkindness of God that is flaming out and oozing all around us as He fathers-forth His glory in the unbroken, unending words and sentences of general revelation. For us to fulfill this calling, and to realize the end of creational theology, we must work at understanding the nature of God's glory, His purposes in revealing His glory, how creational theology serves those purposes, and how we may communicate His glory through our work in this window of theological study.

The Glory of God

Because I have written elsewhere at some length concerning the nature of the glory of God, I will not repeat that discussion here, but merely summarize it.[2] The glory of God is, in essence, the presence of God, revealed to human beings in unmistakable and powerfully affecting ways. Thomas Dubay writes of the glory of God in terms of indescribable beauty: "The glory of the Lord, therefore, is the supereminently luminous beauty of divinity beyond all experience and all descriptions, a beauty before which all earthly splendors, marvelous as they are, pale into insignificance."[3] The Scriptures record that God made His glory known in consuming fires and pillars of darkest smoke; in visible revelations of His enthroned majesty; through the medium of angels; in the Transfiguration of our Lord; in visions, dreams, and visitations of one kind or another; through His creation (as we have seen); and through miraculous works accomplished by His servants. Above all, however, God made His glory known in the Person of His Son, our Lord Jesus Christ, and His work of redemption. His works and teaching provided a foretaste of the most glorious manifestation of the divine presence accomplished in His crucifixion and resurrection. In all these ways God was communicating His presence to human beings, making Himself known and manifest among them, and leading them to respond to Him in extraordinary ways.

The responses of people in Scripture to the glory of God reveal that they were aware of being in the very presence of the God of heaven and earth. Typically, in the presence of God's glory, the first response of people is fear. Then, among those who know Him, fear gives way to praise and thanksgiving, for they understand that, though God is great and powerful beyond everything we know, yet He loves us with an everlasting love, and we are safe in His presence. God reveals His glory to people in order to make Himself known. The objective of this self-disclosure is, as we have seen, to lead people to worship and obey Him and to enter into the rich blessings of His covenant (Rom. 1:18–21). That so few people actually do this does not mean that the purposes of God's revelation are frustrated; it simply proves the teaching of Scripture concerning the devastating effects of sin.

Yet even in the face of human recalcitrance and neglect, God does not desist from pouring forth His glory. His glory is being revealed all around us. It falls to us who know this, and are learning to discern that glory, to point out the majesty, beauty, wonder, goodness, and

205

power of it to those who as yet do not have eyes to see it, or who, having eyes to see, have not begun to discipline them to do so. As we take up the happy task of creational theology and enter more consistently and fully into the glory of God, our own responses of worship and sanctification will provide a foundation and framework for producing theological works—poems, songs, conversations—that can help others to see the beauty of the Lord in the things He has made. Not all will acknowledge that they see Him there; only those who know Him will join us in worship and obedience. Yet those whom God is wooing to Himself may be further drawn to consider Him in His Word, while those who are in rebellion against Him will persevere in that course He has marked out for them, hardening their hearts even more (2 Peter 2:1–3). In every case, therefore, we may have assurance that, as we seek the glory of God in the things He has made and serve Him as docents of that glory, our labors in the Lord will not be in vain (1 Cor. 15:58).

God's Purposes for His Glory

Lest our labors in the area of creational theology become mere exercises in self-indulgence (though what a *sweet* self-indulgence!), we need to make certain that our efforts are in accord with God's purposes for His glory, as revealed in His Word. Thus, we may hope that our work in creational theology will contribute to God's glory being noted and declared, and leading to greater obedience on the part of His people.

That His Glory Should Be Noted

We have argued this point again and again throughout the preceding chapters. God reveals His glory in the things He has made because He intends for people to take note of Him there. It greatly displeases Him, and leads to the pouring out of His wrath, when people ignore His self-disclosures in creation, culture, and the actions of conscience (Rom. 1:18–21). He delights in detailed descriptions of His glory, such as we see in the psalms and prophets. He blesses those who take note of His glory and respond to Him with thanks and praise. Knowing that God's purpose in revealing His glory is that we should take note of it—observing, responding to, and celebrating His glory—must be a guiding factor in our work in creational theology. As we continue to investigate His revelation in creation, culture, and the actions of conscience, and to circle 'round the Creator in all we do, we will fulfill His reason for creating and redeeming us, and for making Himself known in the things He has made.

That His Glory Should Be Declared

But God intends not only that we should take note of His glory, but that we should proclaim it as well, as the psalm that begins this chapter makes clear. All of creation is, as Stanley Jaki insists, but a platform for praising God. As good theologians, we will want to share the fruit of our perceptions and experiences in the book of the world with others of God's people, as well as with our lost friends and neighbors. Again, I want to insist on the importance of producing "theological works" as a result of our labors in creational theology. Even if these works are only in the form of exciting and edifying conversations, they will contribute to God's purpose of declaring His glory to the world. Would we be more impoverished without the poems of Hopkins and Cowper? The music of Bach, Haydn, and Mendelssohn? The illustrations of Jonathan Edwards? I believe we would. Each of us has a contribution to make in this area, if only a "widow's mite." As the Lord did not despise her contribution, neither will He despise our contributions. But we must work hard to make them.

Do not let your work in creational theology end with yourself. There is always someone to talk with about your observations—by now, if you have been doing the activities following each chapter, you know that. Here is an opportunity for you to try your hand in some new area: storytelling, poetry, letter-writing, drawing or painting, even decorating a home or creating jewelry. Your own "theological products" can provide wonderful means of expressing what God is showing us about Himself in the book of the world. Each can be a unique means of sharing your encounters with God and of declaring His glory to the people around you.

That His Glory Should Lead to Obedience

Beyond declaring His glory, however, God intends us to *live* His glory in faithful acts of obedience to His covenantal calling on our lives. Whatever we do, the apostle Paul exhorts us, let it be to the glory of God, so that our very lives become the supreme "theological works" by which the glory of God is made known to the world (1 Cor. 10:31). Daily immersed in and aware of God's glory in the book of the world, and committed to noting, declaring, and living for His glory, even our humblest tasks can become signals of transcendence to the people around us, as Hopkins declared:

> It is not only prayer that gives God glory but work. Smiting on an anvil, sawing a beam, whitewashing a wall, driving horses, sweeping, scouring, everything gives God some glory if being in his grace you do it as your duty. To go to communion worthily gives God great glory, but to take food in thankfulness and temperance gives him glory too. To lift up the hands in prayer gives God glory, but a man with a dungfork in his hand, a woman with a sloppail, give him glory too. He is so great that all things give him glory if you mean they should. So, then, my brethren, live.[4]

Scripture is abundantly clear on what living to God's glory looks like: the fruit of the Spirit (Gal. 5:22–23), the tokens of love (1 Cor. 13), and the holiness that comes from obeying God's commandments (1 Peter 5:1–3). While there are fleeting glimpses of love, peace, integrity, justice, and so forth among the lost men and women of our world, God's purpose for His church is that these attributes, and all those suggested in the preceding references, should abound and flourish and spill over into the neighborhoods of our world from the church of the living God. Thus the body of Christ will rise in beauty—in expressing God's glory—and become the joy of the whole earth (Ps. 48). Thus her enemies will be put to shame, as they will be unable to gainsay her holy, compassionate, and sacrificial ways. Thus our fragmented churches will be drawn into living unity, a unity that can be experienced in spite of important doctrinal differences, as Calvin observed.[5] Thus the purpose of God's glory will be realized as the pagan world is compelled by a glory-observant, glory-living community in its midst to endure the beauty of the Lord day in and day out, like it or not.

Can taking up the happy task of creational theology really contribute to such an end? I believe it can. Our work in this field can dramatically affect the way we live, helping our lives to glow more consistently with the beauty and glory of the Lord. Many matches burning together can make a bright and undeniable light. Our own contribution to this important area may be only a faint glow, but together with the glowing contributions of our fellow creational theologians, it can become a bright light of glory to the watching world around us.

Docents of Glory

Like Edwards, Charles Spurgeon, the great nineteenth-century British preacher, was a noted creational theologian. His sermons abound with beautiful illustrations drawn from his perceptions and experiences of the glory of God in creation, culture, and the consciences of men. The story is told of Spurgeon[6] that he once invited an unbelieving friend to join him on a casual walk through the countryside. The friend agreed, on condition that Spurgeon would not assail him with the gospel of Jesus Christ as they walked. The great preacher agreed, and off they went together. During the walk Spurgeon talked endlessly about the beauty, wonder, majesty, and whimsy of God revealed in the creatures they saw along their way—the trees and flowers, the birds and beasts, and the earth and sky around them. He waxed eloquent, and with evident delight, about the glory of God on display at every hand. Finally, his exasperated friend interrupted and said, "All right, Charles, I see you intend to regale me with the gospel, even without speaking it to me. Go on, then; let me hear it once again, and let's be done with it."

A true docent of glory if ever there was one! Imagine the effect of thousands and millions of the followers of Christ, richly blessed through their work in creational theology, chatting, singing, writing, drawing, living, and working what God has shown them of Himself in the things He has made. How great would be the encouragement to the rest of God's saints! How much more powerful would be the wooing of God's yet-unsaved chosen ones! How forceful would be the evidential power of the beauty of the Lord on those who are hardening their hearts against the gospel! And how wondrously would the purpose of God in making His glory known through creation, culture, and the actions of conscience be furthered on earth, as it is in heaven!

Surely this is a happy task and a glorious promise worth giving ourselves to with determination, diligence, and delight.

Questions for Study or Discussion

1. What will keep you from taking up the happy task of creational theology? Lack of faith? Of time? How can you overcome these obstacles and continue the work you have already begun?

2. Look over the list of books provided in the annotated bibliography. Choose three you would like to read over the next few months. List them below.

3. How will you seek to get others involved in the work of creational theology with you? Start a reading group? Study this book with a friend? Teach it as part of a class? Continue on with your conversation partner?

4. Have you reached the goals you set for yourself for this study? In what specific ways? Where do you still have room to grow?

5. What specific "theological products" will you endeavor to produce from your work in this area? Poetry? Conversations? Let-

ters or e-mails? Sketches or paintings? In the space below, make a covenant with the Lord—like Jacob at Bethel—to honor Him with the work of your hands and mind for what He is showing you of His glory in creation, culture, and the actions of conscience.

The Happy Task of Creational Theology

Activity 9

Continue making entries in your notebook and reflecting on them in prayer before the Lord. Note any conclusions that come to mind concerning the glory of God from your perceptions and experiences. Start making notes as well about the "theological products" you will create to share your observations and conclusions with others.

Meet with your conversation partner and share your answers to the five questions above. Spend some time in prayer together, and finish that time by reading Psalm 19:1–6 and Psalm 8 together.

ANNOTATED BIBLIOGRAPHY

This bibliography is not meant to be exhaustive, but merely suggestive of the kinds of reading that can help Christians to develop the skills and disciplines of creational theology. I have provided only books, although several periodicals can also be useful, such as *First Things*, *BreakPoint Worldview*, *Image*, *Mars Hill Review*, *World*, and *Mars Hill Audio Journal*. I have listed the books by categories, from the easiest and most generally informative to the more difficult and specific. Books that are written from a secular perspective appear in **bold type**. These, as well as all the other books listed below, should be considered carefully in the light of the teaching of Scripture concerning the subjects they treat (Acts 17:11).

General Revelation

Mouw, Richard J. *He Shines in All That's Fair: Culture and Common Grace.* Grand Rapids: Eerdmans, 2001. A succinct and cogent argument for taking general revelation more seriously; also an excellent summary of recent debates on the subject.

Morrow, Barry. *Heaven Observed: Glimpses of Transcendence in Everyday Life.* Colorado Springs: NavPress, 2001. Morrow's wide-ranging survey can be useful in training our senses to discern the glory of God in creation, culture, and the actions of conscience.

Kuyper, Abraham. *Lectures on Calvinism.* Grand Rapids: Eerdmans, 1983. Still useful after a hundred years, this book shows the particular role of Reformed theology in bringing out the glory of God in the fields of creation, culture, and the conscience.

McGrath, Alister E. *A Scientific Theology, 1: Nature.* Grand Rapids: Eerdmans, 2001. A deeper and much more theologically involved study of the subject of general revelation and what is frequently referred to as "natural theology"; very useful for the serious student of creational theology.

Becoming More Mindful

Blamires, Harry. *The Christian Mind: How Should a Christian Think?* Ann Arbor: Servant, 1978. Blamires's arguments about the need for developing more thoughtful Christians are still relevant today, and can provide good guidance in preparing for the work of creational theology.

Noll, Mark A. *The Scandal of the Evangelical Mind.* Grand Rapids: Eerdmans, 1994. A much-needed rebuke to mindless evangelicals, with encouragement that better days may lie ahead.

Langer, Ellen J. *Mindfulness.* **Reading, MA: Addison-Wesley, 1989.** Excellent discussion of "mindfulness" together with guidelines on how to learn to think more clearly and cogently.

Brown, Frank Burch. *Good Taste, Bad Taste, and Christian Taste.* Oxford: Oxford University Press, 2000. Simply the best book on developing the spiritual discipline of taste in the arts; a must-read.

Middleton, J. Richard, and Brian J. Walsh. *Truth Is Stranger Than It Used to Be: Biblical Faith in a Postmodern Age.* Downers Grove, IL: InterVarsity Press, 1995. A good introduction to postmodern thinking and to preparing ourselves as Christians to understand and respond to it.

The Revelation of God in Creation

Hoezee, Scott. *Remember Creation: God's World of Wonder and Delight.* Grand Rapids: 1998. A very good place to begin in understanding why creational theology matters, and beginning to take up this happy task in the realm of creation.

Schmemann, Alexander. *For the Life of the World.* Crestwood, NY: St. Vladimir's Seminary Press, 1988. A very strong argument for a "sacramental" view of the creation—God meeting us there—from an orthodox perspective.

Maatman, Russell. *The Unity in Creation.* Sioux Center, IA: Dordt College Press, 1978. The author strongly argues for the evidence from science of God's upholding presence in the creation, showing how science works and what it can teach us about God's revelation of Himself in creation.

Leax, John. *Out Walking: Reflections on Our Place in the Natural World.* Grand Rapids: Baker, 2000. This collection of essays, reflections, and poems can be useful in teaching us how to be alert to the details of God's glory in the creatures in our own local environments.

Dubay, Thomas, S.M. *The Evidential Power of Beauty: Science and Theology Meet.* San Francisco: Ignatius Press, 1999. Written by a Roman Catholic, this book provides a kind of tour de force of the glory of God in the cosmos, from the far-flung galaxies to the marvels of subatomic particles, teaching us to see and reflect on His beauty in all created things.

Van Dyke, Fred, David C. Mahan, Joseph K. Sheldon, and Raymond H. Brand. *Redeeming Creation: The Biblical Basis for Environmental Stewardship.* Downers Grove, IL: InterVarsity Press, 1996. When we see God's creation as a vehicle of His own self-disclosure, we will want to care for it better; this book is a good place to begin in considering the issues of Christian environmental stewardship.

Polkinghorne, John. *Belief in God in an Age of Science.* New Haven: Yale University Press, 1998. Both scientist and theologian, Polkinghorne teaches us how to consider some of the interfaces between these two areas, with a view to discerning the glory of God being revealed in current scientific discussions.

The Revelation of God in Culture

Niebuhr, H. Richard. *Christ and Culture.* New York: Harper and Row, 1951, 1975. A classic study providing an overview of the way Christians over the centuries have approached the use of culture in the service of God.

Begbie, Jeremy, ed. *Beholding the Glory: Incarnation Through the Arts.* Grand Rapids: Baker, 2000. Helpful guidance from many different disciplines on learning to "read" the arts and see God's general revelation there.

Begbie, Jeremy S. *Voicing Creation's Praise: Towards a Theology of the Arts.* Edinburgh: T & T Clark, 1991. Useful for helping us to see how the arts can play an important role in theological formulation.

Romanowski, William D. *Eyes Wide Open: Looking for God in Popular Culture.* Grand Rapids: Brazos, 2001. Just what it advertises: an excellent place to begin in learning how to look at pop culture for what we can learn about God, His purposes, His truth, and His ways there.

Rookmaaker, H. R. *Modern Art and the Death of a Culture.* Wheaton: Crossway, 1994. This little classic can teach us how to "read" the arts, and the history of art, to discern the ways in which people and societies have either sought or rebelled against God and His truth.

Moore, T. M. *Redeeming Pop Culture: A Kingdom Approach*. Phillipsburg, NJ: P&R, 2003. A helpful introduction to understanding and beginning to appreciate pop culture, with guidelines for growing in the ability to use pop culture for the purposes of God's kingdom.

Acton, Mary. *Learning to Look at Paintings*. London: Routledge, 1997. If we're going to start looking at paintings with a view to discerning their messages, Acton's little book can give us the guidance we need to get started.

Hibbs, Thomas S. *Shows About Nothing: Nihilism in Popular Culture from* The Exorcist *to* Seinfeld. Dallas: Spence, 1999. Very useful in teaching us how to watch television and discern the ways of conscience there.

Johnston, Robert K. *Reel Spirituality: Theology and Film in Dialogue*. Grand Rapids: Baker, 2000. The best way to start learning how to see the revelation of God in film, and to use film as a way of talking about the gospel with others.

Gallagher, Susan V., and Roger Lundin. *Literature Through the Eyes of Faith*. San Francisco: Harper & Row, 1989. The authors provide excellent arguments for reading and producing literature of all kinds as part of our callings as Christians.

Oliver, Mary. *A Poetry Handbook: A Prose Guide to Understanding and Writing Poetry*. San Diego: Harcourt Brace and Company, 1994. Simply the best place to begin in learning to read and write poetry, whether for seeing the glory of God in it or for expressing His glory through it.

Gioia, Dana. *Can Poetry Matter? Essays on Poetry and American Culture*. St. Paul: Graywolf, 1992. By the present director of the National Endowment of the Arts—a Christian and poet—this book shows something of the state of poetry today and of its potential as a means of communicating truth.

Citino, David, ed. *The Eye of the Poet: Six Views of the Art and Craft of Poetry*. Oxford: Oxford University Press, 2002. For anyone interested in learning to read or write poetry—whether to discern the glory of God in it or to express theological conclusions through it—this little book can be a good place to start; with essays from seven poets on the nature of their craft.

Sawyer, Joy. *Dancing to the Heartbeat of Redemption: The Creative Process of Spiritual Growth*. Downers Grove, IL: InterVarsity Press, 2000. Sawyer shows how poetry can lead us to spiritual growth as we read and create it.

Pelikan, Jaroslav. *Bach Among the Theologians*. Philadelphia: Fortress, 1986. An excellent introduction to the use of music in theological formulation, focusing on the "fifth evangelist" and greatest Christian composer.

Wolterstorff, Nicholas. *Art in Action*. Grand Rapids: Eerdmans, 1996. Excellent arguments about the value of art in the Christian community, together with many helpful suggestions concerning ways to express our theological convictions through the arts.

The Revelation of God in the Actions of Conscience

Budziszewski, J. *What We Can't Not Know: A Guide*. Dallas: Spence, 2003. Makes a strong case for the works of the law being written on the consciences of people, and shows how that fact influences everything they do, thus showing us something about God, His purposes, His truth, and His ways.

Wolterstorff, Nicholas. *Reason Within the Bounds of Religion*. Grand Rapids: Eerdmans, 1976. Shows the role of presuppositions—religious preconceptions—in philosophical thinking, teaching us to evaluate philosophical positions for what they show us about the religious perspectives of those who promulgate them.

Van Leeuwen, Mary Steward. *The Person in Psychology: A Contemporary Christian Appraisal*. Grand Rapids: Eerdmans, 1985. A good overview of psychological studies and positions, with an emphasis on how to think Christianly about this field.

Lampman, Lisa Barnes, ed. *God and the Victim: Theological Reflections on Evil, Victimization, Justice, and Forgiveness*. Grand Rapids: Eerdmans, 1999. Guidance on how to think theologically about the actions and consequences of conscience worked out in crime and treatment of victims.

NOTES

Chapter 1: The Inescapable, Inevitable Task

1. Stanley J. Grenz and Roger E. Olson, *Who Needs Theology? An Invitation to the Study of God* (Downers Grove, IL: InterVarsity Press, 1996), 18.

2. Gerhard Ebeling, *The Study of Theology* (Philadelphia: Fortress, 1978), 4.

3. Herman Hoeksema, *Reformed Dogmatics* (Grand Rapids, Reformed Free Publishing Association, 1973), 4.

4. John M. Frame, *The Doctrine of the Knowledge of God* (Phillipsburg, NJ: Presbyterian and Reformed, 1987), 9–10.

5. Helmut Thielicke, *The Evangelical Faith*, vol. 1, *Prolegomena*, trans. and ed. Geoffrey W. Bromiley (Grand Rapids: Eerdmans, 1974), 14–15.

6. Alexander Schmemann, *For the Life of the World* (Crestwood, NY: St. Vladimir's Seminary Press, 1988), 15.

7. Ibid., 76.

8. Frame, *Doctrine of the Knowledge of God*, 333.

9. Ibid., 337.

10. Ibid., 336.

11. James W. Sire, *Habits of the Mind* (Downers Grove, IL: InterVarsity Press, 2000), 135.

12. Cf. T. M. Moore, *The Disciplines of Grace: From Spiritual Routines to Spiritual Renewal* (Downers Grove, IL: InterVarsity Press, 2001).

13. Grenz and Olson, *Who Needs Theology?* 14.

14. Ibid.

Chapter 2: General Revelation (1): An Overview

1. *The Westminster Confession of Faith: An Authentic Modern Version* (Signal Mountain, TN: Summertown Texts, 1979).

2. John Calvin, *Institutes of the Christian Religion*, ed. John T. McNeill, trans. Ford Lewis Battles (Philadelphia: The Westminster Press, 1960), 1.5.1.

3. Ibid., 1.5.2.

4. Ibid., 1.5.4.

5. Abraham Kuyper, *Lectures on Calvinism* (Grand Rapids: Eerdmans, 1983), 125.

6. Abraham Kuyper, *Sacred Theology* (Wilmington: Associated Publishers and Authors, n.d.), 21.

7. Ibid.

8. Ibid.

9. G. C. Berkouwer, *General Revelation* (Grand Rapids: Eerdmans, 1973), 131.

10. Ibid., 131–32.

11. For a most helpful summary of some dissenting Reformed perspectives, see Richard J. Mouw, *He Shines in All That's Fair* (Grand Rapids: Eerdmans, 2002).

12. Scott Hoezee, *Remember Creation: God's World of Wonder and Delight* (Grand Rapids: Eerdmans, 1998), 27.

Chapter 3: General Revelation (2): Two Caveats, Facets, and Goals

1. Thomas Dubay, S.M., *The Evidential Power of Beauty: Science and Theology Meet* (San Francisco: Ignatius Press, 1999), 163.

2. In James H. Trott, ed., *A Sacrifice of Praise: An Anthology of Christian Poetry in English from Caedmon to the Mid-Twentieth Century* (Nashville: Cumberland House, 1999), 195.

3. Alister E. McGrath, *A Scientific Theology I: Nature* (Grand Rapids: Eerdmans, 2001), 291.

4. Ibid., 193.

5. Ibid., 296.

6. John Chrysostom, in Andrew Louth, ed., *Ancient Christian Commentary on Scripture, Old Testament I: Genesis 1–11* (Downers Grove, IL: InterVarsity Press, 2001), 3–4.

7. Richard J. Mouw, *He Shines in All That's Fair: Culture and Common Grace* (Grand Rapids: Eerdmans, 2001), 28.

8. Scott Hoezee, *Remember Creation: God's World of Wonder and Delight* (Grand Rapids: Eerdmans, 1998), 29.

9. My translation.

10. Hoezee, *Remember Creation*, 8.

11. McGrath, *A Scientific Theology I: Nature*, 24.

12. For a most enlightening discussion of the role of popular arts in furthering the Reformation and enlisting people into the worship of God, see Peter Matheson, *The Imaginative World of the Reformation* (Minneapolis: Fortress, 2001).

Chapter 4: Creational Theology

1. Jonathan Edwards, *Dissertation Concerning the End for Which God Created the World*, in *The Works of Jonathan Edwards*, ed. Edward Hickman, 2 vols. (Edinburgh: Banner of Truth, 1974), 1:101.

2. I am avoiding Scripture proofs at this point, reserving them for elaboration in the chapters that follow.

3. David Atkinson, *The Message of Genesis 1–11* (Downers Grove, IL: InterVarsity Press, 1990), 42.

4. Dallas Willard, *Hearing God: Developing a Conversational Relationship with God* (Downers Grove, IL: InterVarsity Press, 1999), 69.

5. Alexander Schmemann, *For the Life of the World* (Crestwood, NY: St. Vladimir's Seminary Press, 1988), 14.

6. See Alister E. McGrath, *A Scientific Theology I: Nature* (Grand Rapids: Eerdmans, 2001), 81ff.

7. Ibid., 132.

8. Fred Van Dyke, David C. Mahan, Joseph K. Sheldon, and Raymond H. Brand, *Redeeming Creation: The Biblical Basis for Environmental Stewardship* (Downers Grove, IL: InterVarsity Press, 1996), 15.

9. McGrath, *A Scientific Theology I: Nature*, 137. Curiously, while McGrath makes a strong argument for looking at nature as creation, he lapses into the language of "natural theology" for the remainder of his work.

10. See T. M. Moore, *Redeeming Pop Culture: A Kingdom Approach* (Phillipsburg, NJ: P&R, 2003), 61ff.

11. J. Budziszewski, *What We Can't Not Know: A Guide* (Dallas: Spence, 2003).

12. John C. Kricher and Gordon Morrison, *Eastern Forests* (Boston: Houghton Mifflin, 1988), 1.

13. Roger Caras, *The Forest* (New York: Holt, Rinehart and Winston, 1979), 15.

14. Ibid., 17–18.

15. Terry W. Glaspey, *A Passion for Books* (Eugene, OR: Harvest House, 1998), 43.

16. Scott Hoezee, *Remember Creation: God's World of Wonder and Delight* (Grand Rapids: Eerdmans, 1998), 31.

Chapter 5: Jonathan Edwards and General Revelation

1. Jonathan Edwards, *Dissertation Concerning the End for Which God Created the World*, in *The Works of Jonathan Edwards*, ed. Edward Hickman, 2 vols. (Edinburgh: Banner of Truth, 1974), 1:101.

2. Ibid.

3. Edwards, Sermon on Psalm 46:10, in *Works*, 2:107.

4. Edwards, Sermon on Psalm 94:8–11, in *Works*, 2:247–48.

5. Ibid., 2:252.

6. Edwards, *Miscellaneous Observations on Important Theological Subjects*, in *Works*, 2:476.

7. Edwards, Sermon on Psalm 94:8–11, in *Works*, 2:254.

8. John H. Gerstner, *The Rational Biblical Theology of Jonathan Edwards*, 3 vols. (Powhatan, VA: Berea Publications; Orlando: Ligonier Ministries, 1991), 1:84–85.

Chapter 6: Jonathan Edwards and Creational Theology

1. Gerard Manley Hopkins, "Conclusion of the Principle of Foundation," in W. H. Gardner, ed., *Gerard Manley Hopkins: Poems and Prose* (London: Penguin Books, 1985), 143.

2. Jonathan Edwards, *Christian Knowledge*, in *The Works of Jonathan Edwards*, ed. Edward Hickman, 2 vols. (Edinburgh: Banner of Truth, 1974), 2:158.

3. Edwards, *The End for Which God Created the World*, in *Works*, 1:100.

4. Ibid., 1:101.

5. Edwards, Sermon on Psalm 94:8–11, in *Works*, 2:253.

6. Edwards, "Sinners in the Hands of an Angry God," in *Works*, 2:9.

7. Edwards, Sermon on Isaiah 33:14, in *Works*, 2:204.

8. Edwards, Sermon on Psalm 46:10, in *Works*, 2:108.

9. Edwards, *An Humble Attempt*, in *Works*, 2:289–90.

10. Edwards, *Notes on the Bible*, in *Works*, 2:697ff.

11. Edwards, Sermon on John 5:35, in *Works*, 2:956–57.

12. Edwards, "Sinners," in *Works*, 2:9.

13. Edwards, Sermon on Romans 5:10, in *Works*, 2:140.

14. Edwards, Sermon on Acts 16:29–30, in *Works*, 2:826.

15. Edwards, Sermon on Romans 3:19, in *Works*, 1:673.

16. Ibid.

17. Edwards, Sermon on Hosea 5:15, in *Works*, 2:830.

18. Ibid., 2:833.

19. Edwards, *Memoirs*, in *Works*, 1:xxx.

20. Ibid., 1:xxxiv.

21. Ibid., 1:ccxxix.

22. Ibid., 1:xlvii.

23. Ibid.

24. Edwards, *The End for Which God Created the World*, in *Works*, 1:101.

25. Edwards, Sermon on Acts 16:29–30, in *Works*, 1:827.

Chapter 7: Practicing Creational Theology (1): Advice from Jonathan Edwards

1. Jonathan Edwards, *Christian Knowledge*, in *The Works of Jonathan Edwards*, ed. Edward Hickman, 2 vols. (Edinburgh: Banner of Truth, 1974), 2:159.

2. Mark A. Noll, *The Scandal of the Evangelical Mind* (Grand Rapids: Eerdmans, 1994), 3.

3. Barry Morrow, *Heaven Observed: Glimpses of Transcendence in Everyday Life* (Colorado Springs: NavPress, 2001), 69.

4. Jonathan Edwards, Sermon on Ephesians 5:16, in *Works*, 2:235.

5. Ibid., 2:236.

6. For additional guidance in learning to use your time more profitably, see T. M. Moore, *Disciplines of Grace: From Spiritual Routines to Spiritual Renewal* (Downers Grove, IL: InterVarsity Press, 2001), chapter 7.

7. Edwards, *Christian Knowledge*, in *Works*, 2:162.

8. For a wonderful series of meditations on how rewarding this can be, see John Leax, *Out Walking: Reflections on Our Place in the Natural World* (Grand Rapids: Baker, 2000).

9. Cf. Ellen J. Langer, *Mindfulness* (Reading, MA: Addison-Wesley Publishing Company, 1989), chapter 5.

10. Edwards, *Christian Knowledge*, in *Works*, 2:162.

11. Ibid.

12. I will mention only a few here; see the bibliography at the end of the book.

13. Edwards, *Christian Knowledge*, in *Works*, 2:162.

14. Ibid.

15. Ibid.

16. Ibid., 2:163.

17. Ibid.

Chapter 8: Practicing Creational Theology (2): Circling 'Round the Creator

1. Abraham Kuyper, *Lectures on Calvinism* (Grand Rapids: Eerdmans, 1970), 125.

2. Alister E. McGrath, *A Scientific Theology I: Nature* (Grand Rapids: Eerdmans, 2001), 159.

3. Stanley Hauerwas, *With the Grain of the Universe: The Church's Witness and Natural Theology* (Grand Rapids: Brazos, 2001), 17.

4. Cf. Dallas Willard, *Hearing God: Developing a Conversational Relationship with God* (Downers Grove, IL: InterVarsity Press, 1999).

5. For an example of this, see T. M. Moore, *A Mighty Fortress* (Ross-shire, Scotland: Christian Focus, 2003).

6. Barry Morrow, *Heaven Observed: Hints of Transcendence in Everyday Life* (Colorado Springs: NavPress, 2001), 16.

7. Richard J. Mouw, *He Shines in All That's Fair: Culture and Common Grace* (Grand Rapids: Eerdmans, 2001), 50.

8. See, for example, A. J. Conyers, *The Eclipse of Heaven* (Downers Grove: InterVarsity Press, 1992), and Robert Wuthnow, *After Heaven: Spirituality in America since the 1950s* (Berkeley: University of California Press, 1998).

Chapter 9: Docents of Glory

1. Stanley Jaki, *Praying the Psalms: A Commentary* (Grand Rapids: Eerdmans, 2001), 49.

2. T. M. Moore, *I Will Be Your God: How God's Covenant Enriches Our Lives* (Phillipsburg, NJ: P&R, 2002), 47ff.

3. Thomas Dubay, S.M., *The Evidential Power of Beauty: Science and Theology Meet* (San Francisco: Ignatius Press, 1999), 45.

4. Gerard Manley Hopkins, "Conclusion of the Principle or Foundation," in W. H. Gardner, ed., *Gerard Manley Hopkins: Poems and Prose* (London: Penguin Books, 1985), 144.

5. John Calvin, *Institutes of the Christian Religion*, ed. John T. McNeill, trans. Ford Lewis Battles (Philadelphia: The Westminster Press, 1960), 4.1.2, 3, 12.

6. Alas, I cannot document this story, but my friend John Armstrong, who knows Spurgeon much better than I, assures me that it sounds "very Spurgeon-like."

INDEX OF SCRIPTURE

INDEX OF SUBJECTS AND NAMES

T. M. Moore is pastor of teaching ministries at Cedar Springs Church in Knoxville, Tennessee. He is a graduate of the University of Missouri (B.A.) and Reformed Theological Seminary (M.Div., M.C.E.), and has pursued additional studies at the University of Pretoria, the University of Miami, and the University of Wales.

He is a fellow of the Wilberforce Forum and editor of its online journal, *Findings*. His column, Ars Poetica, appears on the *BreakPoint* Web page, along with his weekly devotionals.

Moore is also the author of several books, including *I Will Be Your God: How God's Covenant Enriches Our Lives* and *Redeeming Pop Culture: A Kingdom Approach* (both P&R). His book *Ecclesiastes* (IVP) received a 2002 Award of Merit from *Christianity Today*. His essays, reviews, articles, and poetry have appeared in numerous journals and periodicals. He is a frequent speaker at churches, conferences, and seminars.

When he is not working, T. M. wiles away the time listening to Celtic music, reading poetry, playing the mountain dulcimer, and enjoying the glory of God in creation. He and his wife, Susie, make their home in Concord, Tennessee.